Marketing to Libraries for the New Millennium

Librarians, Vendors, and Publishers Review the Landmark Third Industry-Wide Survey of Library Marketing Practices and Trends

Edited by
Hendrick Edelman
Robert P. Holley

Association for Library Collections & Technical Services,
a division of the American Library Association
Published in Cooperation with
The Scarecrow Press of Lanham, Maryland
2002

SCARECROW PRESS, INC.

Published in the United States of America
by Scarecrow Press, Inc.
A Member of the Rowman & Littlefield Publishing Group
4720 Boston Way, Lanham, Maryland 20706
www.scarecrowpress.com

Copyright © 2002 by by Association for Library Collections & Technical Services /
American Library Association

All rights reserved. No part of this publication may be reproduced, stored
in a retrieval system, or transmitted in any form or by any means, electronic,
mechanical, photocopying, recording, or otherwise, without the prior permission
of the publisher.

Library of Congress Cataloging-in-Publication Data

Marketing to libraries for the new millennium : librarians, vendors, and publishers
review the landmark third industry-wide survey of library marketing practices and trends
/ edited by Hendrik Edelman, Robert P. Holley.
    p. cm.
  Includes bibliographical references and index.
  ISBN 0-8108-4271-8 (alk. paper)
  1. Libraries and publishing—United States. 2. Libraries and booksellers—United
States. 3. Acquisitions (Libraries)—United States. 4. Library surveys—United
States. 5. Market Surveys—United States. I. Edelman, Hendrick. II. Holley, Robert P.
Z716.6 .M35 2002
025.23—dc21   2002017586

∞™ The paper used in this publication meets the minimum requirements of
American National Standard for Information Sciences—Permanence of Paper for
Printed Library Materials, ANSI/NISO Z39.48-1992.
Manufactured in the United States of America.

Contents

Preface   v

Part 1: Presentations   1

1 Overview   3
Karen Muller

2 Keynote   5
Rebecca Seger

3 Compare and Contrast: How We Interpret the Results
of the 1999 Survey   7
Hendrik Edelman

4 "Triangle Talk": Publishers, Vendors, and Librarians Speak
out on What the Survey Tells Us about Changes in the
Market and Needs for the Future   15
*James S. Ulsamer, Marty Keeley, Phyllis Young,
Anthony W. Ferguson, Eleanor Cook, and Nora Rawlinson*

5 Selling and Promoting to Libraries: What Are Publishers
and Vendors Doing to Reach Libraries?   33
*Robert Rooney, Alice Peery, Janet Belanger,
Martha Whittaker, and Francine Fialkoff*

6 Cyberspace and Book Selection: How Librarians
and Patrons Are Coming to the Internet to Find out
about the Books They Need 47
Dan Lundy, Peter McCarthy, and Rick Ayre

7 Buying from Publishers and Vendors: A Discussion
among Librarians, Vendors, and Publishers Focusing
on How Librarians Decide to Buy and from Whom 59
*Sarah Michalak, Kathleen Cotter, Rebecca James,
Nancy Pearl, Yvette Berthel Diven, and Peter McCallion*

8 Conclusions 75
Eugenie Prime and Patricia Schroeder

Part 2: Results of the AAP/ALCTS Library Marketing Survey 83

9 Publisher Questionnaire 85

10 Vendor Questionnaire 107

11 Library Questionnaire 135

Bibliography 197

Index 199

About the Contributors 203

Preface

On Sunday, June 27, 1999, the Joint Committee of the Association of American Publishers (AAP) and the Association for Library Collections and Technical Services (ALCTS), a division of the American Library Association (ALA), held an all-day meeting in New Orleans to present and discuss the results of a major library marketing survey. This survey, canvassing by questionnaire the opinions of librarians, publishers, and vendors, followed similar surveys performed in 1975 and 1986. Among the major findings were:

- A majority of the librarians expected their budgets to increase over the next five years.
- Librarians and publishers agreed that much of that increase would be spent on electronic media.
- Electronic media were playing an increasingly important role in the library selection and ordering process.
- Reviews and catalogs, including electronic versions, remained the most effective identification/selection tools.
- A substantial majority of libraries used the services of vendors in placing their orders. About half of the publishers wanted to see an increase in direct orders.
- Almost half of the publishers did not have staff assigned to marketing to libraries.
- Some 20% of the library material budget still went toward backlist purchases.

Panels of prominent librarians, publishers, and vendors reviewed and commented on the findings of the survey. Many commented that the library market was more specialized than the survey data indicated. Much of the discussion was centered on the impact of new electronic technology and media.

Marketing to Libraries for the Millennium: Librarians, Vendors, and Publishers Review the Landmark Third Industry-Wide Survey of Library Marketing Practices and Trends presents the results of this meeting. The book is divided into two parts. The first provides the presentations from the program, sponsored by the AAP and the ALCTS Joint Committee. The second part presents the results of the survey that was the subject of the program.

The survey is the third major marketing survey on this topic. The first two took place in 1975 and 1986. Hendrik Edelman, the coeditor of this volume, gives a brief history of the previous surveys and analyzes the current 1999 survey in chapter 3, "Compare and Contrast: How We Interpret the Results of the 1999 Survey." He is responsible for presenting the results of the survey in the second part and also for compiling a bibliography of publications on the first two surveys.

I was responsible for editing the presentations in this volume. They are edited versions of the ones given at the 1999 ALA annual conference. Some authors prepared written papers, while others submitted an edited transcription of their oral comments. I would like to thank Clint Christensen, my graduate student assistant at Wayne State University, for his transcriptions from the official ALA program tapes. I would also like to thank Michael Rodriguez, graduate student assistant, and Steve Corrsin, assistant director of technical services and head of acquisitions at Wayne State University Libraries, for their help in editing and proofreading the presentations.

The survey and the program at the ALA Annual Conference would not have been possible without the generous support of the ALA; the ALCTS; the AAP, Professional and Scholarly Publishing Division; the Ambassador Book Service; Baker and Taylor Books; Blackwell's Book Services; R. R. Bowker; the Brodart Company; the Charleston Group; Choice; Friends of Libraries, U.S.A.; the Gale Group; Grove's Dictionaries; Henry Holt and Co.; Ingram Library Services; *Library Journal*; McGraw-Hill; Midwest Library Service; Oxford University Press; Penguin Putnam, Inc.; *Publishers Weekly*; Random House, Inc.; *School Li-*

brary Journal; SKP Associates; John Wiley and Sons, Inc.; and Yankee Book Peddler.

Finally, I wish to acknowledge the invaluable assistance of Karen Muller, former executive director of ALCTS, as well as Rebecca Seger and Dan Lundy, AAP cochairs of the AAP/ALCTS Joint Committee during this period. Without their efforts, the survey, the program, and this publication would not have been possible.

      Dr. Robert P. Holley
      Coeditor and ALCTS Cochair, AAP/ALCTS Joint Committee
      Wayne State University

I

PRESENTATIONS

1

Overview

KAREN MULLER

The committee responsible for this program is unique in ALA. It is a true joint committee, being the Library Committee of the Trade Division of the AAP and a similar number of ALCTS members. The committee, which consists of librarians who buy books from vendors and publishers, vendors who buy books and resell them to libraries, and publishers who sell books to libraries and vendors, has worked together for at least three decades. Over those years, the committee has consistently presented excellent programs that serve to improve effective communication, and more importantly understanding of how the library materials marketplace works.

I use the work of this committee on a nearly daily basis, and I am sure many of you do too. The survey being reported today has been done twice before. Twelve years ago, I noted that the 1975 survey had taken place during a time of upheaval in the library market place:

- OCLC was just becoming a national presence—never mind an international organization.
- Minicomputer-based acquisitions systems were still dreams.
- Richard Abel had recently folded, a fact that caused many to question the wisdom of gathering plans.

Then in 1986, we thought we were in a state of unprecedented flux:

- Upstart presses such as Ten Speed were becoming established.

- Self-publishers were popping up everywhere—there was even a new magazine for this group.
- Merger and acquisitions activity seemed rampant, not just on Wall Street but also in "our" industry.
- New forms of gathering plans were being set up, facilitated, and managed with increasingly powerful PCs.

And today, some are convinced that books will disappear. Negotiating licenses or access is a key activity. Mergers and cooperative pacts continue. Again, there is a sense that this survey is attempting to document a dinosaur—the industry formerly known as the book industry, if you will.

But is the book industry dead?

Reviews are still considered important. Publishers would still like to get direct feedback on their list and marketing efforts, but nearly 80% of libraries use vendors for order fulfillment. We continue to predict greater consortia buying. Hardbound books are still preferred to paperbacks. We are finally getting publishers to use CIPs, ISSNs, and ISBNs.

The personal touch is still important, though now it may be mediated by a Web site—and we certainly have learned to control, or harness, telemarketing so it is an asset and not an irritant.

What you are going to hear today will be exciting and important in the fullest meaning of those seemingly trite words. In a paper in a recent *IFLA Journal*, Aad Nuis, formerly Netherlands state secretary of culture and media, wrote a wonderful piece on libraries and the book trade in which he reminded us that: "There is one little thing librarians do not do. They do not, as librarians, bring books into the world. That is the privilege of writers, assisted by publishers, reviewers, sellers of books, all those people that are engaged in the book trade, that risky midwifery that gives a book its public existence in the first place, before it becomes eligible for a place on your hallowed shelves."[1] Today you will look at the life of the book, from birth to taking up residence in your library. Everyone here is a player in the drama.

NOTE

1. *IFLA Journal* 25, no. 1 (1999): 38.

2

Keynote

REBECCA SEGER

Marketing to Libraries for the New Millennium is the culmination of more than two years of effort on the part of the AAP/ALCTS Joint Committee. The committee members represented all parts of what we are calling the triangle: vendors, publishers, and librarians. Equally as important as including all three in the creation of the survey was making sure that the three groups received and responded to the survey.

As Karen Muller mentioned in the overview, this committee has overseen the survey twice before in the 1970s and 1980s. Through the evaluation of the previous surveys, the members of the committee were charged with updating the questions to reflect areas that had little importance then but that have real significance now, such as consortial purchasing of electronic products.

We also wanted to leave enough of the survey the same to be able to contrast the results of this survey with the previous two in order to better understand what has changed in library marketing and what has stayed the same. All the capable past and present members of the committee rose to the challenge of reconfiguring the survey. There have been other surveys developed by one group or another on library marketing or about various publishers. But here we have a group of people who are in the trenches, so to speak, developing, shaping, and creating these questions. Some of these people spend their days dreaming up marketing plans and good giveaways. Others have to respond to these marketing efforts, to answer telemarketing calls from many publishers, and to open stacks of mail from publishers and vendors.

Without the very valuable feedback that came with having committee members who represented libraries, vendors, and publishers, the survey and the resulting program would have been meaningless and very one dimensional. Thus, the overall objective of the survey was to find out about current marketing practices and their effectiveness and about the changes and similarities within the past two decades. Did librarians' responsiveness to particular types of marketing efforts change or stay the same? Did publishers' or vendors' marketing practices change or stay the same as a result of—or despite—the librarians' preferred practices?

The broad survey was meant to reach out to all types of libraries to gather a cross section of opinions. We know there have been significant changes that have affected one type of library more than others such as electronic and information databases and electronic periodicals in academic libraries. But did that really change the fundamental response to book marketing? If so, do the results of the survey vary among libraries so that our next step as a committee should be to survey different types of libraries as a group? This survey is a great starting point.

I would also like to extend my personal thanks to all the members of the joint committee, who despite their own full-time positions, have given their time and expertise to create a survey that could very well influence library marketing for the next decade. I would like to add a special thanks to our program chair Dan Lundy, who is the vice president of marketing for Penguin Books. Through the many hours of work on his part, he has put together a spectacular program with one phenomenal panel after another. I am certain that this book would not have come together nearly as well as it did without Dan's effort.

Our first contributor is Hendrik Edelman. We have the same person who analyzed the survey in the 1970s and 1980s here today to analyze the survey for the 1990s. Henk brings a wealth of experience. He will be retiring next week as a professor of library and information science at Rutgers University. He also held for many years the position of university librarian at Rutgers. Henk will guide you through the maze of statistics as he makes sense out of the mass of data.

3

Compare and Contrast

How We Interpret the Results of the 1999 Survey

HENDRIK EDELMAN

This is the third major library marketing survey organized by the AAP/ALCTS Joint Committee. Previous ones were done in 1975 and in 1986. The results of these surveys drew much attention, both at ALA presentations and in the professional press. A brief bibliography of these and other similar surveys appear on pg. 197.

With change supposedly taking place so fast, is a ten-year period not much too long? Perhaps, but statistical surveys such as these do not necessarily show changes very rapidly. Actually, despite the public perceptions of rapid and continuous change, professional practice changes very slowly on either end of the spectrum.

Good marketing practices for publishers and library suppliers require constant surveys, and, as we will see later, many companies do indeed do that. But a survey like this allows the profession to take stock of the present situation. It creates a common database on which to reflect. Statistics alone are not always meaningful by themselves. While the data may not always show changes very clearly, it is the perspective that informed professionals give to it that provides the added value. Moreover, each generation needs its own data sets to interpret.

Like the two previous surveys, this one was mostly, although not exclusively, concerned with books rather than with periodicals or other formats. There was considerable emphasis on electronic publications without asking, however, for a differentiation in content. In past years, the joint committee followed this survey with one directly concerned with serials.

This survey received responses from 305 libraries, 77 publishers, and 12 vendors. The first two categories were comparable to the previous survey; the response from vendors was half of that ten years ago. This is most probably due to the increased concentration of vendors that has led to a reduction in their numbers. Mergers, acquisitions, and consolidations have diminished the number of major active players.

The responses among the various types of libraries were representative with 35% academic libraries, 40% public libraries, and 20% school libraries. The response rate from special libraries, not surprisingly perhaps because of their diversity, was too low to be meaningful. Among the publishers, the response was 50% from trade, 33% from professional, and some 14% from electronic publishers. There was no distinction made between the various types of vendors.

In their comments on filling out the survey, most participants showed frustration. Because of the level of specificity, libraries found many questions irrelevant or hard to answer. But at least one librarian reported it to be a good learning experience. Publishers were somewhat hampered by the fact that it took many different departments to provide the necessary information, and, undoubtedly, this affected both the return rate and the quality of the answers somewhat.

It has to be recognized that in such a broad, comprehensive survey, the finer points tend to get lost. While, for instance, many library practices are generic to the profession, we all know that there are considerable differences among the various types of academic libraries as well as among large and small public and school libraries, not to mention special libraries. The same applies to publishers. Obviously, STM (science/technical/medical) publishers have a very different marketing strategy than those that specialize in children's books. The data in the previous surveys were disaggregated to a much larger extent, but the complexity of this one unfortunately would not allow that. Therefore, while the statistics are valid, many of the speakers, as they prepared their comments, found it difficult to recognize themselves.

The computer-produced statistics in the report are represented with only one decimal point. Occasionally, therefore, the percentages may not add up to exactly 100%.

While I will most certainly not be the presenter of the 2010 survey, some of these questions will have to be raised by the future organizers.

WHAT ABOUT THAT LIBRARY MARKET?

According to recent figures provided by the Book Industry Study Group (BISG), the size of the U.S. library market is $3.85 billion. Ironically, about the same figure was reported a decade ago. The method of calculation has changed over the past several years and apparently is now much more accurate. Of this amount, academic libraries account for half; public libraries a quarter; while school libraries claim about 15%; the remaining 10% applies to special libraries. A formidable market indeed!

On the matter of library materials budgets, 64% of the academic libraries report increases in the past five years, but some 10% saw decreases. The latter, undoubtedly, is in the realm of small denominational colleges and community colleges. These libraries also reported budget problems in the previous survey. Public libraries fared better with almost 70% reporting budget increases. But clearly troubling is the picture for school libraries. While some 35% reported increases, 22% saw their budget decrease. It demonstrates the ever-growing disparity between prosperous and less fortunate school systems. Fortunately, the poor state of many school libraries has recently been acknowledged in some of our major cities, and help seems now on the way.

Of the current budgets, books make up about a third in academic libraries, two-thirds in public libraries, and about half the expenditures in school libraries. This shows a considerable shift downward from ten years ago. While, at that time, periodical subscription prices were holding down book purchases, especially in the larger academic libraries, it is now clearly the expenditures on electronic materials that are beginning to dominate at the expense of other formats.

This is particularly true for the academic and school library world. Ten years ago, the purchasing of electronic materials was just on the fringe; it is now some 15% of the budgets in academic libraries and in schools. Public libraries still spend most of their budgets on books, periodicals, and other media with only 4.5% on electronic materials. This shift from paper to electronics was predicted in the survey ten years ago, although at that time publishers proved more to the mark than librarians.

It seems important to note that some 20% of the book expenditures are for backlist purchases. Patron requests and the need for replacement copies are most often cited as the driving forces.

When asked about their budget expectations for the future, most academic and public librarians see continuing increases on the horizon, but school librarians continue to be wary. Only 35% expect an increase. But a substantial part, some 66% actually, of the increases will be spent on electronic materials to be bought locally or through consortia. Although it becomes increasingly harder to distinguish between audiovisual and electronic resources in such surveys, it appears that most, if not all, of the increases will go that way. And given the low budget expectations in school libraries, the electronic product is likely to replace the paper ones at a rapid pace.

How do publishers see the future? While the two groups were miles apart ten years ago, it now seems that there is much more agreement. While most publishers expect some increases in book and periodical sales, especially in paperback and children's books, two-thirds of the publishers think that the market for electronic products will increase substantially in the years to come.

WHO RECOMMENDS AND WHO DECIDES?

This seemingly age-old question, so important to those who market library materials, does not appear to come any closer to a satisfying resolution. Actually, the picture has not changed that much since the last two surveys. The truth is that the decision-making process in libraries on what and what not to buy remains murky to outsiders (and often to insiders too!).

There are patterns among different types of libraries, but local practice, often based on traditions and personalities, continues to vary. The issue is a historical one. When library organizational patterns emerged at the beginning of the twentieth century, book selection was not seen as a high priority among professionals. Cataloging, reference, and administration were the recognized specialties. Change has come slowly so that now there are collection development librarians in many larger libraries. They mostly have a coordinating function. The actual process, in most cases, remains a distributed one. That means that recommending, selecting, and deciding are done by many different individuals, very few of whom are identified by job title. Moreover, as personnel changes take place, individual assignments change too. Added to the uncertainty, especially in academic libraries, is that faculty members still have an important say in what is being acquired. Almost half of the academic libraries report faculty selection as a significant factor.

A rather new reported phenomenon in the selection and decision-making process is the practice of group decision making. This is especially true for periodical subscriptions and electronic resources. This is understandable because there are many aspects beyond content and price that have to be taken into account. Such groups often include selectors, catalogers, reference librarians, order librarians, computer staff, and administrators. Obviously, this process tends to slow down the decision making.

For publishers contemplating this market, there are no quick and easy solutions to identifying the individuals most likely to play a deciding role in the selection process. As we will see later on in the survey, some do it well, and some do not, with many still considerably confused.

SELECTION TOOLS: ANY NEW TRENDS?

Compared to the earlier surveys, librarians appear to be much better prepared for the decision tasks. Across the board, 80% of the libraries report to have collection development plans in place. Such documents usually are blueprints of the libraries' intentions and indicate their strengths and areas of major concentration.

Most librarians continue to rely on reviews in deciding what to buy. An overwhelming 84% reports so. The library and book trade reviews score highest, but it is interesting to note that online reviews have entered the marketplace as well. Publishers report that any review is better than none but that a negative review does affect sales to libraries.

A large number of librarians also report reliance on publishers' catalogs. In general, librarians prefer to know about new books some three months prior to publication date. Online publishers' catalogs and publisher Web sites now draw some 40% of the librarians' attention.

Of lesser importance, but nevertheless of use as reported by a third of the librarians, are direct mail, national and regional exhibits, media coverage, and author appearances. Space advertising, especially in the review media, is frequently mentioned. Although of greater use in academic libraries, blanket orders and approval plans continue to have an impact on the selection process.

Among the least favorite methods reported are publishers' sales calls and especially telemarketing calls. More than 85% of the librarians do not like telemarketing. This is a similar response compared with the previous survey. At that time, however, publishers put a very high value on this strategy. Nowadays, the publishers appear more experienced and more selective in the choice of telemarketing targets.

HOW DO PUBLISHERS AND VENDORS APPROACH THE MARKET?

Remarkably enough, only half the reporting publishers have a person directly responsible for library marketing. Half of these, only 25% of the total, have an actual sales force.

This means either that publishers, assuming that wholesale orders constitute the market place, do not know or care about the library market or that they do not know how to approach the market. It is somewhat disconcerting that after so many years of effort by the joint committee so many publishers do not pay attention to the library market.

But the good news is that, more than in the previous surveys, the publishers who do market to libraries are doing it much better. They like to use focus groups, mail and telephone surveys, advisory boards, informal visits to libraries, discussion lists, and, above all, contacts at conventions.

Moreover, the active publishers appear to be much better in tune with the market than before. Their opinions on the effectiveness of selection tools parallel those of librarians. They also seem to put their advertising dollars where the market is.

Not surprisingly, virtually all the reporting vendors have a marketing staff, some indeed quite extensive. Vendors report that more than 75% of their budget goes to sales representatives and national exhibits. This is a clear indication of their priorities. Their bibliographic services in alerting libraries about needed materials are seen as most effective through the use of online publishers' catalogs and Web sites as well as through various blanket order and approval plans and e-mail notification of new titles.

PLACING THE ORDERS

The proper identification of the person in charge of actually placing the orders remains a problem for publishers and vendors. Yet it is a very important question. Depending on the size of the library, this could be the library director, the acquisitions/order librarian, or someone else. There are no clear organizational patterns in any of the libraries. The same problem applies to the person who decides which vendor to use. In most larger libraries, this is now, however, a group decision, in which many interest groups are represented.

Not surprisingly, a majority (77%) of the libraries place their orders through vendors, but they also order directly. Although the report cites only a small percentage for orders placed through online bookstores (1.9%), it is clear from listening to librarians and booksellers that the Internet is rapidly changing library practice.

Some 45% of the publishers would like to see an increase in direct orders from libraries, but an equal number express no preference. The dichotomy in the industry thus continues.

Vendors and publishers report that price, including discounts, remains the strongest incentive for the direction of library orders, but speed of delivery, service quality, and online capabilities are very important as well. Librarians confirm this.

In the service area, returns are unfortunately still an issue. Among the reasons cited, receipt of defective items remains high. But so are duplicate shipments and duplicate library orders. It all adds up to a serious waste of time, money, and effort.

INFORMATION TECHNOLOGY IN THE ORDERING PROCESS

The automation of library operations has been in process for over thirty years with a great deal of success in standardization. It is perhaps surprising, therefore, that many libraries have not automated their internal services, including some 25% of the reporting academic libraries. But even more surprising, that same group apparently has no plans to automate in the near future. This certainly has some consequences for vendors. It also points to the fact that there is a substantial gap between the haves and the have-nots that should concern the profession.

All participants in the survey report that the use of CIP, ISBN, ISSN, and other common industry standards continues to be considered of great importance.

We have already mentioned the increased use of the Internet in various library procedures. Virtually all reporting libraries have Internet access.

A somewhat new wrinkle in the ordering process is the use of credit or debit cards to speed up payment and to simplify procedures. The survey is not clear on this, but anecdotal evidence points in that direction, including reports of staff members volunteering their personal cards for increased frequent flyer mileage! This practice is another question for discussions about the code of ethics.

EXTERNAL FACTORS

The issue of outsourcing has received much attention in the past few years. This survey shows that the practice is more diversified. Within academic and public libraries, a high percentage uses approval plans of one kind or another. Only 25% of the school librarians do so. Many other forms of outsourcing are popular, such as book processing, cataloging, binding, and so on. In the electronic arena, leasing rather than purchasing has become a more common practice.

Consortia promoting various aspects of library cooperation have been around for a long time, but the notion of common purchases is relatively new. The survey shows a high percentage of libraries active in one or more consortia, but the report shows still limited activity in purchasing books and periodicals. The use of consortia for the purchasing of electronic products, however, is now very common. Several of these consortia have been founded in recent years for that purpose alone.

There is much food for thought and discussion in the report, and I look forward to the rest of the program where many prominent practitioners will give their views on the results.

4

"Triangle Talk"

Publishers, Vendors, and Librarians Speak out on What the Survey Tells Us about Changes in the Market and Needs for the Future

JAMES S. ULSAMER

When asked to put together a presentation for this panel, I had sixty-three pages of tabulated survey responses so that the challenge was how to compress something like that down to five to seven minutes. I thought I would take a topic that may not be of much interest to many people, but I would then see if I could do something with it anyway. I will thus discuss trends in Internet usage and the implications for the future of libraries, vendors, and publishers.

Here are a few responses from the survey relative to Internet usage. Currently, 11.2% of library budgets are now spent on some type of online products and services. But more significantly, 51% of libraries say that online expenditures will be the greatest area of increased spending in their budgets in the next five years. What does that tell us? It tells us that usage will continue to grow at a rapid pace.

There are also questions about the effectiveness of the Internet as a sales and promotional tool. The survey responses certainly support the Internet's use in that area as a growing trend. Forty-one percent of libraries rate online publishers' catalogs and Web sites as highly effective promotional tools. There is agreement among the vendors since 72% of them rated Web site and online publicity and information as important in influencing vendor selection. In addition, 63% of the vendors rated databases as highly effective in promoting to libraries. They feel the Internet has a high priority for promoting to libraries and for also influencing from whom the library orders. Furthermore, it is interesting that 45% of the library respondents rated Amazon.com and some other Web sites as highly effective review sources. Let us take a look at the implications of this fact in that it is no great secret that more vendors and publishers will emphasize Web sites to promote their products and offerings.

As you have seen, databases have become richer. Keyword searches, tables of content, reviews, annotations, and other features have been added to databases. I don't think it will be too far down the road when we start seeing more and more things like first chapters and even full text of reviews. These additions will be potential marketing tools to help prospective buyers decide if they want to buy a book. It will probably work best for higher-priced books. What I really think is most interesting, if you believe the statistics, is that traditional review sources may be somewhat threatened. I think that people post reviews of books on Web sites for the general public and that people read them and place some credence in them. Yet we are still used to the review sources that we value, whether they be the *Library Journal* or a variety of other sources. What is happening is that the fickle consumers out there are imposing their opinions and thoughts on the whole process. That will continue to have an effect on how we should promote to our customers and satisfy libraries.

Regarding the Internet as an advertising medium, I pulled out one response that showed that 38% of the library respondents rate Internet sites as highly effective advertising tools. *Library Journal*, which has very broad-based penetration within our community, came in at only 48%. I do not mean to pick on *Library Journal*, but it is a highly visible promotional resource within the library community. I think the implications here are that traditional advertising vehicles and revenue streams could be at risk. The fact that the public is responding to advertising on Web sites will shake up some of the traditional structures we have in place.

The library acquisitions process is going to continue to experience change. Two-thirds of the vendors indicated that they now offer some type of online Internet access for ordering. Approval plans and standing order plans were rated high in effectiveness by vendors in promoting and selling books to libraries. Furthermore, 36% of libraries accessed the Internet for out-of-print books and backlist titles as well as for titles difficult to find in traditional sources. One last statistic under this general topic is that 70% of the libraries in consortia purchasing groups claim that they obtain better discounts and better pricing of electronic services and that they intend to continue to participate in such arrangements in the future.

Now what is this likely to mean in the acquisition process? Obviously, Internet-based ordering will continue to grow. We have received the message from our customers that the Internet is the preferred way to place orders. I think that more automatic shipment services will be offered via the Internet. Right now, there are standing order, approval plans, and other Web-based services. I think that the Internet will allow us to go far beyond that and to get into areas such as author plans. The library usually knows how many copies of a best-selling author that it will want to receive. We can set those things up. Likewise, award winners, whether they be state or national winners, can be profiled on the Web for review so that the library can make the choice whether or not to order those books. Furthermore, I expect that the Internet will continue to provide better access to and more efficient procurement of hard-to-find products. A lot of the out-of-print books and hard-to-find books are now easily available on the Internet from various dealers. Until today, there was no efficient way to find out about these products.

My last point is that consortial efforts in the future will be more successful in getting price improvements on online products and services. The main reason is that there is a high fixed cost of creating these online services, but the variable costs for additional users are much lower. Thus, there is more incentive and practical business value in offering price breaks on online products as opposed to products like books that carry a much higher variable cost. You quickly run out of room to further discount print products.

To conclude, I will throw in a few other predictions about the future based on the survey results and increased Internet usage. I believe vendors, libraries, and booksellers will play a major role in e-book distribution. There needs to be an aggregation of the availability of these products. Patrons will come into the library or their bookstore where they don't want to search for a Random House book or an Oxford University book. They will want a book by a subject or by an author so that this whole process will have to be aggregated. Vendors will have a role to play by being a conduit for delivering electronic products from the publisher to the end user.

Worldwide Internet access to book databases will dramatically alter and is already altering the international rights system. If you are a consumer in

Germany and log on to a database where you see a book you want that is published in the United States, you don't really care or know that there might be territorial rights somewhere else. That has already begun to reshape the rights systems. I think we will end up with a system that is arranged more by language than by geography. Books will continue to be sold more freely across territorial boundaries. That has already happened in the last few years. With access to data, customers—whether non–U.S. nationals wanting to order books from the United States or U.S. citizens wanting to order books from other countries—know that these books exist and will be asking for them. This factor will create demand for ways to deliver books across international boundaries.

Publishers will find it beneficial to use wholesalers to distribute to direct-marketing customers. What has happened is that wholesalers have demonstrated their ability to drop ship on behalf of a bookseller so that a publisher could mount a Web site and, instead of dealing with day-to-day fulfillment, have those orders shipped straight to the individual or institutional customer. We have thought about this possibility at Baker and Taylor for quite a while, and I believe this may happen. Book databases could very well form the platform for retail up-selling. We say this because, if you look at all the information that mankind has accumulated over time, no one has organized it, managed it, and put it in an accessible manner better than librarians, and that is why many databases are based on subject categorization. It would be a logical process for someone to do a search about a subject. These people could then find a book, but the subject database could also be a platform to bring in other retailers to sell products relating to the subject that interests the potential customer.

MARTY KEELEY

I am the president and CEO of Ingram Library Services. There are twelve business units in the Ingram Book Group. Please don't confuse me with the book company. I don't say that in a negative way. We are different. Now that I have delivered my commercial, I can begin my comments.

As Jim Ulsamer mentioned, wondering what to say in five minutes with sixty-three pages of data is always a formidable task, but when following your former boss and chief competitor, there is always something to comment about. Specifically though, I'm going to bounce around and talk about the subject at hand: the change in the market and the needs for the future. What we are consistently hearing, and I think the survey bears this out, is that it's more, it's faster, and we need it better. That is very, very profound insight from this survey.

Henk Edelman mentioned marketing research. Yes, we do constant market research, just like everyone else. Have we spent $2 million to hire a consultant to go out to gather information for us? No, we haven't. We base a lot of our intelligence on going out and spending time with librarians, patrons, and publishers. Henk also mentioned, and it's obvious in the survey, mergers and acquisitions. As an organization that has just come through seven months of an unsuccessful attempt at a merger and acquisition, I can tell you that mergers and acquisitions are here and will continue to happen. I think you will keep on seeing consolidations in all facets of the bookselling marketplace.

Working with publishers, specifically in marketing, is important. Our core competency is distribution. We pick them, we pack them, and we ship them. That's what we do. We work very closely with publishers. For the publishers in the audience, if you're coming to ALA and you're not spending time at Ingram Library Services, you're making a very serious mistake. We depend dramatically on the publishers to help with our marketing documents and our catalogs.

Regarding the reviews, and Jim mentioned those very quickly, I must say that *Library Journal* was the real winner in this survey regarding the use of that particular channel for print. Since reading the survey, I am questioning, and our director of marketing is questioning, some of the things that we are doing in our company. Specifically, we are looking at the statistics for the vendors and the reaction from the librarians regarding the exhibits as they are currently in progress downstairs from this meeting room. Maybe exhibiting is not the best way—we may be spending too much money doing that. Concerning sales representation, it was somewhat alarming for me to see that most of the respondents see sales representatives as glorified customer service reps. That was not good news for me.

Let us talk about the "O" word: outsourcing. We have to discuss it. It is like discussing the facts of life with your children—it is something that you need to talk about. All I will say is that we do it; we are guilty of outsourcing. Every six months, we are seeing a doubling in the processing services that are required by our company. I don't think that it is anything to be ashamed of in the sense that you need it more, better, and faster. What we are trying to do is help you satisfy your patrons and your customers.

I will make some predictions while I am up here. I think that the survey shows that competition is good. There are more full-service wholesalers and vendors out there today trying to help you do your jobs than ever before. I think that competition has raised the bar for all of us who are in distribution. I think it is safe to say that we are all working harder to satisfy your needs and to meet your requirements.

The last prediction I will make is that these e-books are here to stay. They are coming faster than even you may think or than I may want to believe. There are libraries out there buying multiple copies of e-books, to test them, to taste them, to feel them, and to touch them. There are people working on every facet of the e-book revolution and on enhancing the capabilities of these e-books. They're coming, and they're here.

I will conclude with some remarks about the Internet. It is my goal in the year 2000 to stop printing so many catalogs, advertisements, and fly sheets and to get as much as we possibly can up on the Internet because librarians are telling us that this is what they want. I think it is interesting that we deal specifically with public libraries at Ingram Library Services. I must be fair and say that academic librarians led the way, but I think public librarians followed very closely behind. I want to see much more about us on the Internet, a development that will save us a lot of money from not having to print as many materials.

PHYLLIS YOUNG

As a collection development librarian, I was asked to talk about the survey in relation to new options for collection development. One interesting finding in the survey is that most libraries now report that they have access to the Internet. That means that in the library we have access to tools that we have not had before now. Plus, we have the impact of our customers coming to us and accessing some of the same things that they see on the Internet. That impacts the choices we have to make, especially when we have survey data that show static or decreasing budgets for some institutions.

But as a practicing collection development librarian, I think one thing that I have noticed in the last couple years that is really changing quickly is having access to information for all kinds of materials and in all formats that we can then use in the collection development process. Some of that information was previously difficult to find. My staff and my collection development friends across the United States are saying that we are relying on these new automated tools to do our jobs. Twenty percent say they use the Internet always or often. Another 35% say they use it sometimes. That says something about the way our jobs are changing. I see this as positive for selection. It enables staff to make better choices and to manage budgets more effectively, especially when these budgets are not as robust as we would like them to be. Mine certainly is not.

I find it fascinating to hear people talk about how they are using the titles of information from these electronic sources, manipulating them in ways that fit their needs, and then sending them back to staff. This is especially true for those of us who have decentralized selection. In this way, they can use available information to make better choices from their limited budgets. I see the options becoming even more varied over the next few years. I would also say that things that I wished for when I became a social science evaluator are things that I am finally beginning to see happen. As a customer using Web-based products, I think my staff are asking for more electronic sources. The more information you put up from wholesalers' products, as well as from publishers' and their Web sites, the better the options for getting information to do effective collection development.

I would like to comment next on automated ordering since the findings were of interest to me because automated ordering is impacting what I do. While our ordering process has always had automated elements to it, we are currently planning and implementing an automated process for acquisitions in our library. I found the statistics interesting about the number of libraries that do not have any automated ordering processes and are not planning to implement them. I am not quite sure what that means other than that a lot of respondents were from smaller institutions. But I do think that, as it becomes easier for us to transfer information electronically, we are all going to want to do so because we will get materials to our customers faster that way. I guess my plug here is that I would like to see the wholesalers work as closely as possible with the automation vendors that provide our integrated library systems in order to help us expedite this process. We keep hitting blocks as we try to figure out how to fix certain things and to improve the automated ordering process. This is a major change from what we are doing.

I am a book person. I always tell my librarians that. Even though I am deeply involved in electronic online database purchasing to the point that they think that this is all I talk about, I still think that books have a place and a role in a library. I also think that e-books are going to be something that gains the attention of the library market. All of my collection development librarians attended BookExpo America this year; the one thing every one of them mentioned in a discussion after the conference was e-books. I am not sure, however, what we are going to do about e-books. We are not there yet, but e-books are coming. We are going to have to deal with them.

I am interested in another area of the survey: change in the way we look at paperbacks, trade paperbacks in particular, because I see the same thing happening in some of my libraries and think that this change must be common for other public libraries as well. Some of the statistics indicate that the importance of paperbacks might be increasing for public librarians or that they are at least looking at this option. I know that in my library, if given a choice, my branch staff often prefer a trade paperback over the cloth edition. This choice also has something to do with the limited budgets that we have. As I am reminded more and more every day, many titles are coming out only in trade paperback. The latest Clive Cussler series is a good example of a new series that will appear only in trade paperback.

The survey responses about promotional materials were interesting to me since obviously I deal with such materials quite a bit. I find it worthy of note that the traditional options are rated quite highly. I was also glad to note that tables of content and reviews remain highly important for us. As automated products become available to us, I hope that tables of content and reviews will still be there for us among the options to get the information needed for effective collection development.

ANTHONY W. FERGUSON

Like the other panelists, I was asked to talk about what the survey tells us about changes in the marketplace. I will speak from the viewpoint of someone doing collection development work in an academic research library. I have found my assignment somewhat difficult because 75% of the respondents to this survey were not university librarians. The results are better for public, school, and two-year colleges.

I will, however, comment on what I believe to be the case in research libraries in one area of the survey where the market is changing radically: digital forms of information. Specifically, I will discuss (1) the significance of online materials, (2) who has the selection responsibility, (3) information about new titles, (4) the importance of discounts, (5) the potential for renewed interest in backlisted and reprinted titles, (6) the role of vendors, and (7) the overpowering role that licensing and copyright issues play in collection building.

The Significance of Electronic Resources

It is significant that, even for all libraries, this 1997–1998 survey indicated they were spending 11.2% of their funds on local or remote online resources. But the key phrase for research libraries is: the more digital resources, the better. If that is not true for every research library today, it will be tomorrow. We have just experienced an avalanche in the number of serious e-journals. We are beginning to hear the sounds of the next avalanche in which e-journals are linked to online reference tools and to each other. Further up the mountain are electronic monographs. While it is easy to question the range of contents of early efforts like Netlibrary.com, for the student who wants information, full-text searching of a large body of digital monographs beats eye-scans of thousands of pages of disorganized books found through browsing or library catalogs. Students want information, not monographs.

Selection Responsibility

In this area, the survey results for research libraries are not as helpful as might be wished. The survey is concerned with the importance of the head librarian versus others working in the library when selecting materials. For digital materials, research libraries are in chaos compared to the good old days of print acquisitions. Previously, you selected a title on the basis of user need and the strength of your budget. In the case of collections, you might have given passing thought to how technical processing might be effected. The "you," however, was typically singular—whether head librarian, subject specialist, or faculty member—one person was making the decision. Now the "you" of collection development involves a variety of people with differing needs and points of view: the library systems office, whose machines and systems are needed to access and use the information, wants to give input; the public service department, which provides printing or downloading help, wants to give input; the acquisitions department, which has all sorts of new procedures that must be followed, wants to give input; and, of course, the selectors want to give input. All of these participants demand to be involved. Vendors and publishers need to figure out how to contend with their needs for participation and information.

Information about New Materials and Publisher Promotional Materials

The current survey suggests that catalogs (getting 35% of the votes) and reviews (64% of the votes) are the most important sources of information about new publications. Sales calls, on the other hand, got only 5.6% of the votes. For digital materials, the opposite is usually the case where catalogs without a sales call are not particularly useful. Reviews are still important for digital sources of information, but the important ones no longer appear in print. Rather, new sources of digital information are informally reviewed behind the closed doors of discussion lists not open to publishers and vendors. While sales promotions happen formally in the context of meetings of the International Coalition of Library Consortia and similar meetings of regional, state, and local groups, librarians often put out the word about what the vendor representative said as soon as the representative leaves the building after doing a demo. Since vendor representatives often schedule visits to different libraries on successive days in the same week, we often know what was talked about and are ready to ask the same questions, to push on the same issues, and then to compare notes with each other.

The Importance of Discounts to the Acquisition of Digital Forms of Information

The survey reflects the importance of consortial purchasing agreements with 42.5% of the responding libraries indicating they belonged to two or more purchasing consortia and 70.3% of these indicating they belonged in order to get "favorable pricing for electronic products or services." Indeed, aggregated consortial pricing for digital forms of information is practically a given for most digital titles. The importance of discounts is of course nothing new. Libraries do not expect to pay retail bookstore prices. But since so much of what is purchased is paid for annually, librarians find it incumbent to work with other libraries to obtain the best discounts. In my own institution's case, the price for the major package of databases we purchase through a consortium annually is 25% less than retail. Without this discount, we would buy 25% less than we do.

The Potential for Interest in Backlisted and Reprinted Titles

The survey shows 79% of the libraries spending less than 10% of their budgets on backlisted materials and only 8% frequently buying reprints. I have an idea that, in at least the immediate near future, recent and long out-of-print books will prove to be of critical importance as monographic publishers clamor to put together packages of digital books. For electronic periodicals, it has been a given that journal back runs are important. Digital versions of out-of-print monographs will serve the same purpose. One needs only to look at what is included in Netlibrary.com to see how this is true.

The Role of Vendors

The survey indicates that 78% of the materials acquired by libraries come through vendors. This is also true for one area of digital purchasing: electronic indexes, abstracts, and other reference tools with vendors like First Search, Ovid, and Silver Platter. For full-text journals, however, this is less the case. Publishers seem to want to hold on to their content. This is unfortunate since this means users have to learn many different interfaces. There are exceptions like the German STM publisher, Thieme, who is trying to get its content into as many third-party systems as possible. Netlibrary.com seems to be the only vendor in the full-text monograph business. This is unfortunate. I hope things will change. I dread the thought of dealing with hundreds of publishers and their lawyers over licensing and copyright issues. Without the help of vendors to overcome these problems, the nature of collection development work will increasingly require less and less content expertise and more and more copyright training.

This Is a Good Segue into a Few Final Comments on the Overpowering Role of Licensing and Copyright in Today's Libraries

The survey is largely silent on this issue. Yet, my selectors and I spend inordinate amounts of time working on licenses or kibitzing about licensing principles and practices. Publishers, vendors, and librarians all seem to be the captives of copyright laws and lawyers. We are all sure that everyone else is out to get us; and we intend to do unto others as we expect they will do unto us—except we'll do it first. And given the speed at which our institutions are getting into the distance education gold rush, licensing issues will become even more important as the days roll by.

So what have we learned about the future of marketing to libraries is that:

1. Digital is becoming supreme—although books will continue to be purchased.
2. Selection is complex, and vendors/publishers need to work with all kinds of people in each library.
3. Sales calls are more important now than in the past.
4. Libraries want a lower per unit cost of information and are organizing to force vendors and publishers to respond.
5. Since people want information, backlists of out-of-print books are very important.
6. In this complex world, vendors are critical in helping navigate the chaos of the digital world.
7. We seem to be in the clutches of an octopus called copyright, and we all want to escape.

These are exciting times, and we need each other. If nothing else, this survey helps to bring publishers, vendors, and librarians together.

ELEANOR COOK

I am pleased and honored to be a part of this panel. I do not have a formal paper to read to you. I thought that I would listen intently to my colleagues here and then try to hit some of the high points and make comments about some of the trends that the survey has identified.

As Hendrik Edelman mentioned when he opened, the survey has been done three times. I think that, as we start looking toward the future for new surveys, we might want to look at how we are doing these surveys. I did think that the survey was helpful. I have always been an amateur trend watcher. The survey is useful as we think about ways to do things in the future.

One of the things I think we should do is focus on finding out more about the specific characteristics of different market segments. Several people noted that academic libraries, public libraries, school libraries, and so on sometimes come at these things a little differently. Since a majority of the people that responded to the survey are from smaller libraries, I think that we have to acknowledge from where they are coming as well as from where we are coming. In regards to that, I come from a medium-sized academic library. Many of the comments that Tony Ferguson mentioned certainly are similar to my experiences.

I have a different spin on one of the comments that was made regarding automation in acquisitions processes as seen from the results of the survey. I feel that, though some public libraries have no plans for automation, the companies they work with and that supply them with library materials are automated. These small libraries depend on their company's automation to fill their orders. Furthermore, if you are at a very small branch of a public system, you may send your orders to some central office where automated acquisitions processing will be found. Thus, I do not think that these libraries are not affected by automation but that, at their size level, they might not need it.

Another comment is about credit card usage. There was a very interesting program yesterday morning that was sponsored by the acquisitions section of ALCTS. The University of Delaware discussed how it implemented a policy and practice of using credit cards. I still think that many people that are using them are using them for special and rush orders as opposed to using them for everyday bulk ordering. But with the rise of bookseller services on the Internet, I think we will see an increase in credit card use. This usage is really more as a purchasing card than as credit card. Many of us have started using debit cards, instead of checks, so I think that this will happen in our work environments as well.

Let me touch on a few things that each speaker said. I think that Ulsamer's comments about effective review sources are interesting. I think review sources are extremely important and that the formal reviews that we expect to see in places like *Library Journal* or *Publishers Weekly* are still relevant to us as librarians. What you see on Amazon.com is what individuals are thinking about the book they read. That might be useful to you as a consumer, but, as a librarian, we still want to see formal reviews. I do think that many review sources are going to move to the Internet and that in the future you are not going to see people flipping through reviews on *Choice* cards. But today our collection development specialists still enjoy doing that. I think the trend will take hold slowly but that it is going to happen.

I do think that publishers and vendors are making strides in providing us with functional Web sites where we can go to look at their entire catalogs and order directly from them. Progress in the usefulness of Web sites has been slow in the past. Everybody had to have a Web site, but you couldn't do anything with these sites; you just looked at them. You saw them load, but they did not have much functionality. There are a lot of improvements in that area. As many of you know, I am editor of an online discussion list called ACQNET; and I partner with Anna Belle Leiserson, who maintains AcqWeb. The growth of the number of publishers and vendors who are linked to AcqWeb has just been phenomenal in the past three years so that it is a good place to shop for different vendors and publishers.

Marty Keeley mentioned some of the differences between the pick, pack, and ship services and also talked about, I think, the academic booksellers in the market. We are used to a type of customer service that goes beyond the basics. We have come to expect a lot from our vendors. The vendors we typically use are going through merger mania right now; we are going to have to watch to make sure that customer service is still there.

I have to say that it is very important that we continue to have good customer service with electronic products. One of my frustrations as a serial specialist right now is that I am trying to take advantage of the so-called free e-journals that come with a print subscription, but I cannot get anyone at the publisher to call me back or answer my e-mail so that I do not know how am I supposed to link to free e-journals. It is very important to me that there be someone on the other end to talk to.

Another issue that Tony Ferguson alluded to was the importance of copyright. This is a tremendously important part of what is happening during the transition. Because of the copyright issues, I think that publishers need to allow vendors to help them distribute their electronic materials. We don't have time to continually pore over licenses and sign them one by one. We need to find blanket license agreements that are standardized where we all promise that we aren't going to misuse your material. Since we don't have to sign a license every time we buy a book, we shouldn't have to deal with licenses if we are buying things piece-by-piece on the Internet.

I also think another important aspect of copyright is cyber rights for authors. There was a very interesting article in *Publishers Weekly* on June 14, 1999, that talks about the transitions in cyber rights. I suggest you take a look at this article if you have not seen it already. I think we are going to find not only that are we going to have to look at each publisher, but also that we are going to have authors who are not willing to give up all their rights.

NORA RAWLINSON

It is exciting to be here today. I applaud the joint efforts of the AAP/ALCTS Joint Committee to bring together publishers, vendors, and librarians. One of the disappointing things that I often find at ALA is that there is so little opportunity for publishers and librarians to speak to each other. The notable exception is publishers who publish specifically for libraries and those people who work for trade publishers whose job it is to market to libraries. I have to say that publishers generally have no idea about who you are or how you buy. Many times they throw up their hands and say: "There is no way to influence or to reach this market."

When Fred Ciporen began his job as publisher of *Library Journal*, he was amazed by this realization and began to call libraries the invisible market. He said that if you talked to most people on the street and you said the word "library," they would respond, "books." But if you talk to New York publishers, they would respond, "Baker and Taylor." It is perfectly all right to have distributors that work between these two areas, but the problem is that publishers are then quite a distance from the market, do not really understand it, and cannot learn to love it or publish for it.

When you look down at the exhibit floor, it is very interesting to see how much is electronic. Yet, when we look at the survey, libraries are still very much in the book world. How little of the exhibit floor is dedicated to adult books. Children's books are still pretty strong, but there is little in the way of adult books being represented. Thus, I think it is extremely important that a survey like this be done. However, I also wear a hat as someone who speaks to a lot of publishers. I am searching desperately to hear somebody who is in charge of library marketing talk to the head of their company about who reaches and influences librarians. I am afraid my lack of results is a bit discouraging.

One of the most discouraging comments I heard from the panels today was Marty Keeley's saying that, when he took a look at what librarians were saying about what influences them, ALA exhibits rated very low. In fact if you look at the ALA exhibit numbers and the results when librarians were asked to respond from one to five about what is most effective to least effective, 48% say that exhibits were either least effective or next to least effective. I think this is a problem with librarians. It is the chicken and the egg dilemma. Librarians are not spending enough time on the exhibit floors; therefore, the exhibits cannot affect their buying with the result that more publishers will not come to exhibit at ALA. This has been part of the reason why, while I have been at *Library Journal* and *Publishers Weekly*, I have encouraged librarians to attend BookExpo America (BEA). It was very exciting that Phyllis Young talked about her entire staff going to BookExpo America. It was in Los Angeles so that she was able to send them all. It is important for librarians to be at BEA to talk to publishers about what they are buying and what they are interested in. Publishers cannot be aware of your presence unless you are there talking to them. That may bring them to ALA as well so that the ALA exhibits will have more influence.

In the survey, librarians responded in such a way that the publishers might as well give up advertising title listings. Fifty-five percent say that advertising was the least effective method of reaching librarians. I think librarians are missing a real bet if they are not paying attention to publishers' advertising. Of course, you have to read advertisements with professional judgment by using all the tools you were taught in collection development classes, but this is a method for picking up on things that you might have missed. I often remember Richard Ford. When his first book *The Sportswriter* came out, it got terrible prepublication reviews. I didn't buy it for the Baltimore County Library. It wasn't until I heard that *Time* magazine and some of the other magazines that I hadn't looked at had given it good reviews that we bought it. You need to second-guess what is going on with the reviews. Reviews came out in the survey with extremely high marks as being influential for librarians in terms of buying. I was very interested that so much is being discussed regarding the Internet's role in regards to selection of information. The Internet is becoming a very interesting place.

Many of you may be aware that Amazon.com got its hands slapped by the *New York Times* where an article pointed out that placement on Amazon.com's front page and its *Books We're Reading* list was often paid for. From a bookselling perspective, this is not a shocking idea. Amazon.com is a combination of a bookstore and a provider of information about books. In a bookstore, it is very common that the books that are on tables and in the front of the store are paid for to be placed there. For Amazon.com., it makes sense for publishers to pay for that type of placement in their virtual bookstore. Thus, we are getting this combination of editorial and sales promotion on sites. Librarians are going to have to be careful about how they understand information on places like Amazon.com. There is also going to be an interesting fight between how editorial and advertising are presented on all types of Web sites. There is a lot of concern in *Brill's Content* magazine in the current issue that talks about this blurring of advertising and editorials. This blurring is potentially a big issue.

It has also become clear from everything that people have said that libraries have their feet in both the print world and the electronic world. This obviously creates problems for budgets, how you deal with your patrons, and how you understand what your patrons are looking for. This is an extremely great challenge for all of us. Tony Ferguson mentioned the whole issue of the book as a format. This is an interesting concept for us to think about. He said that students are looking for information and not for monographs. The book has been a wonderful format for particular purposes, but we have been forced to use it for others where it is not the most effective format. For example, the book is not really all that useful for discrete bits of information.

Electronic sources are a lot easier to use. There are ways in which one uses a book that sometimes are not the most convenient. The example was used of traveling and having to carry a whole stack of books when it would be a whole lot easier to carry the Rocket E-book, which I have right here, loaded with lots of information. This way you don't have to be pulling out a lot of different books to help you in your travels. In this way, we are beginning to understand how the book is a format and how electronic sources are better for some purposes. The book is still going to be ideal for fiction, but for sources of discrete information I don't think the book is the best format. I think we already knew this from how difficult it was to learn how to use book indexes and how much we had to study in reference classes to learn how this particular reference work was ideal for this and another was ideal for that.

The other thing I found interesting was the growth in the trade paperback format. The good news I have for you is that publishers are going to be producing more trade paperbacks. It is the one real success area in terms of sales. While mass-market paperback sales have been declining, trade paperback sales have been growing substantially. This has been attributed to a lot of different things, not the least of which is Oprah Winfrey and her reading club because many of the books that she selects are trade paperback format. The hundreds of thousands of reading groups that are developing in the country have really brought the trade paperback format to the forefront.

Tony Ferguson also mentioned, as did several other people, about discussion lists becoming an interesting hidden review process. That worries me. I think that we need to open up these lists quite a bit more to publishers and to the rest of the world. First of all, we know that crazy rumors develop on the Internet. Do you remember Kurt Vonnegut's supposed speech that went all over the Internet? We then found out that it wasn't Vonnegut's speech at all. This kind of thing can develop on discussion lists too. They need to be open so that publishers can learn from you about what you are expecting in terms of books and other formats. It is also necessary so that people can correct each other when rumors develop.

Of course, there is the whole issue of copyright. Eleanor Cook mentioned the analogy that we in libraries do not sign copyright agreements for the number of times a book gets borrowed from the library. I will point out that this is not true in every country. For example, in Britain they sample which books circulate, and the government pays authors for the fact that these books have been used multiple times. What is going on in copyright as far as I can tell is that all the interested parties are trying to correct what they regarded as the problems of the past. Writers feel that they never got enough money for their books. Publishers feel they never got their fair share either. And in the new electronic world, all parties are going to try to solve their problems. The analogies to the past aren't really going to work. We're going to have to argue things in brand new ways.

5

Selling and Promoting to Libraries

What Are Publishers and Vendors Doing to Reach Libraries?

ROBERT ROONEY

I should preface my remarks by saying my background is in general academic publishing, not scientific publishing, of books and journals. There are many librarians for whom my usually biased remarks will be eschewed. When I was going through the survey, it was difficult to pick out many patterns that really jumped out at me. One that I could see was that librarians, no matter what type of library they worked in, can't stand to talk to publishers. I can't say that I blame you. You weren't so crazy about some of the vendors either. I can also understand that. When I came to the part where you said you were dubious about coming to shows like this and speaking with one another, that finding really confused me.

I have a few points to make here that result from my specific publishing background. Some publishers, especially reference publishers, really do try to get the initial sale since there is continuity in sales after contact has been made with the first sale. That is true for journal publishers as well. But we as publishers can also accept the important role of the vendor. A question for me as we go forward is how we can get closer to our customers, that is, you librarians, by working with our vendors.

When I first started in this industry, getting any information beyond the fact that vendors were selling books and journals to libraries was impossible. Learning the identity of those libraries from the vendors was totally out of the question. This has changed over time, but, as I see us going forward, I think we need to collaborate more about the sharing of information about who those customers are, how they are reacting to both the types of products and to the specific medium the products are offered in, and how we can better service those end users. I can see that librarians are going to need vendors in perpetuity.

This brings me to my next set of reactions to the survey. I think the survey respondents from libraries did not appreciate the impact that consortia are going to have in the next ten years within the tripartite relationship of publishers, vendors, and librarians. I think consortia will fundamentally change part of the way the relationship is currently structured in regard to the facilitating role that the vendor currently provides. There are many different types of libraries out there so that publishers don't all have the resources to manage the best way to market to all of your needs. That is where the vendor provides the greatest service.

But in the consortial relationship, especially for journals but also for books, libraries are aggregating and coming together as one voice and want some additional price break as a group. The reason for part of the price break we give vendors—though not the sole reason they get a discount—was because they were the aggregators. Now it doesn't make any sense to have two aggregators. From a publisher's point of view, should the discount, which we used to pass on to the vendor who sorted out issues for us in dealing with libraries, get shifted to the consortia? If the consortia come directly to us, what becomes of the role of the vendor for the publisher and indeed for the consortia? This is not a rhetorical question. In my ignorance, I don't have the solution to give today. I see that as a fundamental problem for the tripartite relationship as consortia begin to emerge.

Finally, I would like to discuss the tremendous growth in the desirability and usability of online services that the survey indicates have become so important for virtually all libraries to purchase to meet their user needs. Again in relation to vendors, whether they are subscription agents or wholesalers, how can publishers collaborate more effectively to shape the online information that we can give you up front so that you can make informed purchase decisions? When you go to third-party sources for information, are there any quality control checks? If you come to the publisher and the publisher has it wrong, well it might not be surprising, but it shouldn't happen. What if you go to a third party who makes representations about the availability of products from publishers that frankly are based more on the third party's business practices than what is sitting in the publisher's warehouse? I think that everyone needs to know that those things are going on. Those were my principal reactions to the survey.

ALICE PEERY

I am approaching these issues from a practitioner's perspective in a large- to medium-sized public library. Since there are many libraries in this category, they represent a sizable proportion of library buying power. Public libraries were the greatest percentage of libraries responding to the survey, but the responses were mainly a snapshot of small public libraries. In looking at larger- and medium-sized public libraries, or even systems with more than one library, the responses would have been different.

Video and sound recordings, music and spoken audiotapes, circulating software, and new formats such as DVDs are becoming an increasingly important part of public library collections. They are now considered a basic service. They are not luxuries to buy only if there are extra dollars. Patrons expect these items to be in the collection.

The survey focused on the head librarian as the principal selector. This is true for small libraries, but the larger the library system the larger the number of methods used for selection. More public libraries are moving to various types of centralized selection because it gets items the public wants on the shelves much faster. It is possible to select centrally without sacrificing the quality of the collection. In many ways, centralized selection can make a collection more current.

One surprising response from the survey was a lack of interest in electronic ordering. Public libraries, especially those with more than one location, need automated ordering. They need electronic ordering that has an interface with the local automated system so that the act of placing an order encumbers funds and places titles in the public access catalog. Patron holds, an essential public library service, may then be placed on titles the day that they are ordered. Automated ordering that does not have an interface with the local system is not very useful. Public libraries are looking to vendors—not to publishers—to provide this service.

Another surprising response was the lack of interest in preprocessed materials. Having items shelf ready, particularly for nonprint materials, is becoming more important. Since public libraries need more public service staff, one way to provide them is to deploy support staff to public service functions. Outsourcing cataloging and processing, traditional technical services functions, is a way to reassign support staff to the front line. It is more efficient to manage outsourcing through one vendor rather than through multiple publishers.

Trade shows were not ranked as important in the survey. Trade shows are very useful to public libraries. Regional shows are important because many public libraries do not have large travel budgets. The shows are a good opportunity to look at books, particularly reference sets. They are also useful for looking at new electronic products. It is expensive to bring an electronic product in on a trial basis because a large number of staff needs to review it. It is more useful to take a quick look at a product at a trade show to determine whether or not it is worth bringing it in on a trial basis.

The survey focused on reviews as a major tool for marketing to libraries. Reviews are important; however, many of the most used subject areas, such as job hunting and business plans, are not adequately covered by review sources. Relying solely on review tools would leave major gaps in a public library collection. Publishers' promotional tools are more important now than they were even three to five years ago. Vendor print tools are also useful because it is easy to cover a number of publishers by using them.

Since public libraries do not collect comprehensively, they need a thorough description or annotation, preferably with any review citations, for titles under consideration for purchase. It is necessary to know the scope of a title and whether it is the type of book needed on the subject. *Books in Print* is just a starting place to identify a title. Public libraries need additional information before purchasing.

A publisher's Web site would be an ideal place for this descriptive information on backlist titles. The new online vendor products are also helpful for information on backlist titles. Public libraries buy a number of backlist titles, both for replacement purposes and to fill gaps in subject areas. In fact, one way to fill gaps in a subject area is to review the titles of a specialized publisher. A well-designed and informative Web site would facilitate such a review. The publisher who can provide information on backlist titles will have an edge and will sell more of them. This is also a good marketing strategy for publishers because, in most cases, backlist buying is for multiple copies.

The survey did not rank a publisher's reputation as important, but it is. When considering a title without a review, the publisher's name and reputation can make the difference in deciding whether or not to buy a title. A quick review of the publisher's Web site can often provide enough information about the publisher's quality.

One strong point in the survey responses was publishers' expectations that libraries will increase their direct orders. Public libraries, however, are not likely to decrease ordering from vendors for two reasons: the need for electronic ordering that has an interface with the local automated system and the need for shelf-ready items. In addition, direct orders are expensive because they are so labor intensive. It is a lot of work to create and receive a purchase order for a few titles that might be purchased from a vendor as part of a larger purchase. Because of this, it will be difficult for publishers to know their customers with more public libraries' buying from vendors. Thus, one challenge in the next few years is for publishers, vendors, and libraries to forge the necessary communication links to understand each other's needs.

JANET BELANGER

It was no real surprise that the most popular marketing tools are still print catalogs, flyers, and reviews, just as they were in the last survey. Complete catalogs and subject catalogs are favored over other kinds of mailings. Traditional library review sources such as *Choice*, *Booklist*, and *Library Journal* are still the most popular, with *Publishers Weekly* not far behind. Electronic media really have not made inroads here—yet.

At the opposite extreme, libraries rated telemarketing as one of the least effective marketing methods. However, there is a difference between the cold call, where the telemarketer quickly begins to read from a prepared script, and the call from a publisher or vendor, with whom we have an ongoing relationship, who is calling to update us on something in which it has reason to think we will be interested, given its knowledge of our needs and past business experience with us. The former type of call is generally not useful at all, particularly in larger institutions where placing orders is a process with checks and balances. It is highly unlikely that any one person called in these libraries has the authority to both make a selection decision and place a purchase order. Also, particularly in an academic environment, targeting the call is a major issue. Trying to sell an acquisitions librarian on the value of a major publication in an esoteric subspecialty of biomechanics is far less effective than calling the library liaison to the biology department, or better yet, one of the biology faculty members.

Calls from known representatives are often welcomed as a heads up on new products and perhaps an opportunity to touch base about other ongoing business with that vendor or publisher. We may not really think of these latter calls as telemarketing calls while publishers and vendors often think of them as such. That may be one possible explanation for the discrepancy in the importance placed on telemarketing by each group in the survey.

Libraries did not rate exhibits very high on their list either, with the possible exception of state and regional shows. Of course, part of the reason for this is accessibility. Many librarians have neither the resources nor the ability to attend ALA or other conferences. Meetings such as the Charleston Conference, for example, are smaller gatherings focused more on continuing education than on selling and buying. Certainly exhibits are used by libraries without approval plans as a means for gaining some hands-on exposure to titles of interest. Those with approval plans may also take the opportunity to review the more expensive reference materials that may not be included in their approval profiles. Also, as the electronic media portion of the market continues to grow, exhibits are one of the best ways to see a variety of products, to be able to compare similar products, and to have hands-on access, which is not always available during in-house demonstrations.

Sales calls from publishers were not rated all that highly in terms of usefulness. In the academic market, where many libraries receive a majority of their domestic and perhaps many of their foreign books through blanket orders and approval plans, publisher visits are not quite so vital, particularly when looking at new publications since they tend to come automatically. However, this is not as true for electronic products where demonstrations by vendor representatives are vital. Also, visits from vendor representatives were ranked equally low—a puzzling finding. Vendors' visits are important to outline new services, to demo new online databases, and to troubleshoot problems, particularly for new accounts. Again, because academic libraries tend to rely on approval plans and blanket orders, these visits are vital for the establishment and ongoing maintenance of these plans. Also, as libraries rely on their vendors for preprocessing and provision of cataloging, the need for open lines of communication are only increased, particularly at the start of the plan. While we may often feel that these visits take a chunk out of our day, the importance of developing working relationships with our vendor representatives cannot be taken for granted. Often, the success of our relationship, particularly with a vendor, is directly related to our ability to sit down and communicate our needs and expectations. The best time to do this and to guarantee undivided attention on both sides is through a vendor sales call.

Consortia or purchasing groups were not listed as a means for promoting products or services. Perhaps in the future they will need to be. At least half of the respondents reported obtaining better discounts for print material through a consortium or buying group. Many of us are buying the majority of our electronic products through consortia or some other type of like-minded group. In some cases, we will steer a representative to our consortium director in order to obtain potentially better discounts or terms for a product in which we know others in our group are also interested.

Web-based catalogs and databases are clearly a new favorite. To think they weren't even on the survey twelve years ago! Librarians, publishers, and especially vendors all rated them highly as a marketing tool. Certainly, the amount of time and investment in developing and promoting these pages is not being wasted. Going to a publisher or vendor page to obtain information rather than tracking down that catalog or piece of paper you know you filed somewhere is certainly an attractive and convenient option. The ability to order or claim online is also a great convenience. As more of us are able to easily cut and paste or otherwise download data to our ordering system, these databases will become great time savers and vital tools in our daily work flow design. Also, to a small extent so far, e-mail is being used as a means for announcing new publications and special sales. While spamming is not welcome, these announcements, again from vendors and publishers with whom we have ongoing relationships, are useful and convenient for redissemination to other interested parties in our organizations.

Another factor in the use of Web-based information resources is the extent to which our user base—faculty and students in the case of an academic library—are comfortable and conversant with the technology. Tools such as Amazon.com and other resources for purchasing books online provide useful information, but they also raise expectations. It is difficult to tell faculty members that it will take a week to ten days to obtain a title from a vendor or publisher when they respond that they can obtain it in a few days from their favorite online purveyor of books. While few respondents are using the online bookstores at present, one reason may be the need to use credit or procurement cards that are not yet widely available to libraries.

While the two extremes—catalogs and reviews as most effective and telemarketing as least effective—have not changed much in twelve years, a newcomer, online resources, has made impressive inroads. Just as we saw no discussion of the Internet and Web resources in the last survey, I suspect in ten more years that more of the survey will be given over to those forms of communication and access, or at least to whatever their next incarnation will be.

MARTHA WHITTAKER

I work in the Blackwell's marketing department. It is a position that I have held less than two months so I am pretty new to this world. I do have some observations about the survey. I am going to second a lot of things that I have heard from this panel and from those who spoke earlier this morning. About two months ago when I started with Blackwell's, I hired an independent research firm to do some market research, primarily having to do with the merger of my former company, Academic Book Center, with Blackwell's.

During the lunch break, I met with the woman who is doing that research for us. She told me the things that she is finding, but they are very different from the things I have found in this survey. Of course, as you know, 75% of the respondents to this survey were public librarians. My market is overwhelmingly academic libraries so that colors my remarks. It may also account for the difference in the findings.

I was interested in the fact that 46.2% of the respondents said that discounts are the most important factor in deciding on a vendor. I understand that everyone is very cost conscious these days. They also rated service and online capabilities as very important. We have heard from all the librarians that have spoken today that the services that come from book vendors are very important. Eleanor Cook was quoted as saying: "We've come to depend a lot on our vendors." We heard the same comment from Phyllis Young. Yet, I was struck by the fact that 45% of the publishers in the survey say that they really prefer selling to libraries directly. There is a little bit of a disconnect in these statements.

During the question-and-answer period, this morning, Phyllis Steckler from Oryx said something that I thought was absolutely true. She said: "The real increase in direct selling is not publishers' selling directly to libraries but publishers' selling directly to consumers and users." I think that she is absolutely right. I don't really consider that I sell books. I sell all the services that wrap around the books. They are very expensive services. One of the things that strikes me is that we as book vendors need to be better not just at marketing the value of those services but at making people understand those services.

A number of people have said today that the Web tools that vendors have developed for managing approval plans, ordering, and so forth are very expensive to create and maintain. Yet, it is interesting to me that these services that differentiate one book vendor from another are the very things that we give away. We get money for books, which in our world are really a commodity. Our market of libraries can buy books from a lot of different places, but our services differentiate us—and we give them away. I don't know if that is a sustainable business model. The marketing implication for me is that we need to do a much better job of making both publishers and librarians understand the value and the cost of the services that we provide.

I would like to comment a little on sales calls. I thought it was interesting that the survey respondents rated sales calls as very low. I cannot believe that they mean traditional book vendors. Just as Janet Belanger said, we sell approval plans. I cannot imagine selling an approval plan without extensive sales calls. Again, the survey did not seem to connect with my experience. This is certainly not something we would cut back on as a result of this survey. In order to sell the types of services that book vendors sell, our sales force is really the most important part of our marketing and sales budget. Just as Tony Ferguson said that the sales rep is extraordinarily important in selling electronic resources, it is also true in selling book services.

Moving on to electronic resources, a lot of people said that e-books are here to stay. Tony Ferguson said that for full-text monographs we will need the vendor. He also said that students want information, rather than monographs. It was also said this morning that, in many respects, the book is not the best medium for obtaining information. The electronic book changes all that; it makes it much easier to aggregate pieces of information. As Tony said, we need our book vendors to be involved in that process. This is not a marketing thing, but it is a perfect lead up to what I have to say now.

Just today at this conference, Blackwell's Book Services and Net Library have announced a partnership so that Blackwell will be distributing in the academic market the e-books of Net Library. We also will have an opportunity to work with Net Library to assist it in its collection development policies and to go together to publishers to talk about the possibilities of digitizing popular and not so popular reference works. It is interesting that we have come to realize that monographs come in many formats. They come in hardbound, paperback, the U.S. edition, and the Braille edition; and now they also come in an electronic edition. A book vendor needs to be able to say to our approval plan customer and to our permanent order customers: "You can have whatever format you want including the electronic format."

One final observation as I get back to the survey. I, too, was interested in the comment about the amount of backlist buying. Backlist and out-of-print have tremendous implications for book vendors. I think we need to be looking carefully at the on-demand printing services. I would like to see my own company establish a relationship with Ingram, Lightning Print, Sprout, or one of the many on-demand printing services. Those are my impressions. Thank you very much.

FRANCINE FIALKOFF

I almost feel like the summarizer since the panelists have reiterated so many of the same points. The previous surveys of this publishing triangle, though they were a decade apart, were valid for twenty years because things did not change that much during this long period. Today, however, we are on the crux of huge technological changes. More of our business is going to be done on the Web. This survey can only be a snapshot of this point in time. A lot of the things said today about things that will happen are going to be coming really fast at us. Some of the things in this survey that are true today may perhaps not be valid for very long.

Before I address the future, I want to talk about some points from this survey. I think some of the panelists have already said them as well. This is a relational business. Librarians don't find out about books through osmosis or just through vendors. Nor do they find out about them just through reviews because, if that were their only source, they would be aware of only about 10% to 15% of the books published. They find out about books in a myriad of ways.

Publishers are not marketing to libraries. In fact, the survey indicates that the number of people in publishing houses who are responsible for marketing to libraries has dropped from 60% in the last survey to a rate of 44% in this survey. Marketing dollars aren't being translated into library marketing even though large percentages of publishers' titles are being sold to libraries. The survey indicates that 35% of publishers reported that over 40% of their sales were to libraries; 23% of them said that libraries account for over 60% of their sales. That is fairly substantial. Yet 29% spend less than 10% of their marketing dollars on libraries. Fifty-four percent say that less than 20% of their marketing dollars goes to libraries. I think there are some disconnects here where some people are not realizing that you have to market to libraries in order for them to know about your books. There are many ways this can be done, and many of the panelists have discussed a number of these ways. Just hoping that you are going to get a review or that a vendor will list your books in the catalog isn't good enough.

I think that the reason for this is the disconnect that has been going on for years between publishers and librarians. I am sorry to see that it is still so apparent in the numbers. I think publishers are missing opportunities to get to the end user, something that publishers want so desperately. They are moving a lot of advertising dollars over to consumers, but consumers buy more than the best-sellers. They buy a whole range of books.

I would like to throw out some numbers: 65% of the American people use libraries; 80% of those people go to libraries and come home with a book. Libraries can be used as marketing tools because people who use libraries are also book buyers. Surveys have shown that. I think publishers are being shortsighted in underutilizing libraries to market books. I hear librarians complain all the time that they cannot get authors into their libraries because publicists are so taken with the idea of getting their authors into the superstores.

Every librarian and author that I have talked to has said that more books have been sold in libraries, either through the library's selling the book or the bookseller's collaborating and bringing the books into the library. A publisher program at a Barnes and Noble might have authors sell five or so books; but, at the library, you can sell many more books. It is an excellent way to market your books. The library doesn't just have a sign in the window or hand out a flyer on the day the author is going to be there. The library has a publicity machine. It sends out newsletters. It gets media attention for its authors. It plans huge events.

David Domkoski of the Tacoma Public Library was telling me that he has difficulty in getting authors to his library, but, when he does, he can attract six hundred people to the event. At the local Barnes and Noble, they are unlikely to get twenty-five people. I wish there were a way to get this message out. Unfortunately, though we are speaking to each other all the time, we are obviously not hearing or listening to each other. I don't know where the disconnect is or how to get things changed, but something is dysfunctional here.

I know that Carol Alabaster at the Phoenix Public Library just started a program a year ago, when their new library opened, for bringing authors into the library. She has had huge success. She sent a media kit to New York publishers and has got a lot of authors to come out there. She had a one-day science fiction festival where I think she sold $3,000 worth of books in that single day. She also has smaller programs as well. If publishers used libraries more, perhaps they would know a little bit more about what goes on there. I think there is a much bigger promotional picture than we are currently seeing.

Reviews ranked high for selection, but I want to remind you that perhaps only 50% of the books in this country get reviewed. Janet Belanger asked if we would do more reviewing if we could review online. The answer is yes—theoretically. I think that, in the future, it would be wonderful if we could review every book that came out. Of course, we would have to pay the editors and have space at an overhead cost. I think that no matter how wonderful my publisher is that we will not find the money to be able to do that quite yet, but it is something that we are thinking about more often.

We are also thinking about reviewing electronic books. I am getting calls from authors who want to know our policy on reviewing e-books. I say to them that we are developing one right now. I think things are changing very rapidly. Bob Rooney was talking about the fact that, because his titles are academic and specialized, people do not learn about them. If you were to wait for the academic journals to review them, you could wait from six months to a year or more. Thus, he has to get the word out in other ways.

A number of publishers that I spoke to said that advertising was a necessary evil. If you looked at the survey, you might think that librarians never looked at advertising. The librarians on this panel will certainly tell you otherwise. It is ironic that, though the numbers are really low in the survey when it comes to librarians' rating advertising as an effective vehicle, nevertheless, when they were asked which publications they ranked highly as advertising vehicles, they were very quick to answer. More than 50% of them had an opinion about which of the publications they liked, and they ranked them very highly. They were not all talking about *Library Journal*. For not being interested in advertising, librarians seem to know a lot about it.

As it is for many of you, the Net is changing us at *Library Journal*. We have just started an e-mail newswire for academic libraries because we realized we weren't covering that market very well and that no one else out there was covering it well either. From the publishers' end of it, there is a very big news component so that we have started a prepublication alert on some books. Right now it is a fairly small component of what we're doing, but we intend to expand it. I hope that the academic publishers out there will let us know about their titles. We would especially like to learn about "hot titles" from academic publishers four months before their publication. If the editors know about a really great story behind the book, please tell us. If you just won an award, let us know. In fact, I think that we are starting to change in this area toward the way things will be.

6

Cyberspace and Book Selection

How Librarians and Patrons Are Coming to the Internet to Find out about the Books They Need

DAN LUNDY

I'll be talking about cyberspace and book selection: how librarians and patrons are coming to the Internet to find out about the books they need. Before you hear from the speakers, I will first give a short bit of scene painting.

When we met as a committee at the ALA annual conferences and midwinter meetings to talk about a new survey, we decided early on that one of the major changes in marketing since the last survey in 1987 was the explosion of the Internet. The New York Public Library Web site gets an astonishing ten million hits per month; it is an affiliate of BarnesandNoble.com. Discussion lists are now well established among librarians. We sent an e-mail press release for this program to serialists, AcqWeb, Publive, Medlive, Pwdaily, Booklife, Edupage, and so on. Thirty-five people exchanged nearly five hundred e-mails in order to make this happen because we live all around the county.

We decided that the 1999 survey had to ask publishers, vendors, and librarians about how they are coping with cyberspace. How are publishers and vendors incorporating this new technology as they launch new titles and keep old books before the public's eye? To what degree have librarians hopped on board the information highway to provide the books they need and to keep up with their patrons' requests? The survey gave results about many of these issues.

The vast majority of libraries now have Internet access. Seventy-seven percent of responding libraries say they order through vendors partly to avail themselves of cataloging and processing services, but no doubt also to use online catalogs to check bibliographic details and to learn in a timely fashion about best-seller lists, award winners, Oprah selections, and to find out about authors on tour that might spark demand for certain titles. AcqWeb lists thirty-six hundred publishers internationally, and it now has comprehensive lists of online serials and reviews for all types of books.

The survey reported that online booksellers have a modest 2% or less of their sales from libraries. The traditional print review media prevail over online reviewing. We strongly expect that this picture will change rapidly. Online sellers now have about 15% of the consumer book-buying dollar according to some research. That has been very explosive growth. Lest we forget, one-third of the books that are read come from the library. Twenty-two percent have been borrowed by a friend or a family member according to the Book Industry Study Group.

The survey says that 20% of the budgets for library materials are earmarked for purchasing backlists, replacement copies, and patron requests. The Internet is a godsend for describing and selling backlists. On-demand printing will soon help acquisitions people and vendors to get those fill rates even higher. The survey found that 41% of responding librarians thought Web sites and online catalogs were important for library marketing. Sixty-three percent of the vendors felt that they were very important. Both librarians and publishers agree that more dollars will be spent in the future on electronic media.

PETER MCCARTHY

I have a quick anecdote from my flight to New Orleans from New York. On the plane, I was trying to sleep; sitting behind me were librarians and other people coming to this conference who were working in the book industry in different capacities. As I was drifting off, I kept hearing three words: Internet, Web, and cyber. I did not get a lot of sleep on the flight when I realized that I needed to shed light on this subject today. To that end, let me launch into my presentation.

Forty-one percent of responding librarians consider online publishers' catalogs as important. This is the statistic that I found most interesting in the survey. I am probably going to have a slightly different take on it from the people that have been speaking today. From a publisher's perspective, that statistic may appear great. However, from someone working in new media who has a mandate to increase publishers' Internet presence, I find that number very low. My inference, and this is an amusing hyperbole for illustration, is that while the Internet has entered our collective unconscious, it has yet to become a major tool. It is still a tertiary tool. It is something people turn to as a secondary source. They are still using our hard copy catalogs from what I hear, and I'd like to change that. Not only does using the online publisher's catalog cut down on mailing costs, it also cuts down on your need to organize files of publisher's catalogs.

I would like to say just a couple things about how publishers view the Web. I would also like to give some likely reasons why the library community has been slow to adopt publishers' Web sites and why this is also true in the book reading community as a whole. The very first thing publishers thought about the Internet was that it was a marketing tool and little more than that. The first sites were basically publisher catalogs placed online. There was no use of the added capabilities of the medium except perhaps for a subject searching key. Publishers' sites were not interactive. For the most part, they were static, and you could be sure that, if you went to a publisher's site, you would have to look at advertisements during the time you spent there.

As the Web matures, so will our attitudes and our actions. With the proliferation of online booksellers, the world has caught up with the Web, particularly our world of selling books. There is the common quote that "information wants to be free." My little joke is that books do not. We recognize that the Web is very powerful. We definitely see ourselves in the world of business. A friend coined the phrase: "We are purveyors of the reading experience." We make books. We have a lot of our money devoted to editors whose job it is to find these books and to edit them once we have acquired them. Basically, we are producing the books that wind up in libraries and bookstores. That's our business. When we look at the Web, we obviously look at it as a marketing tool. But I want to emphasize in my talk that we are trying to look at something more than that. I think that it is in this area where you will all see some changes in book selection.

My comments will be broad. I don't mean to advertise for Penguin Putnam, but I know their sites better than other sites. The last time I checked, most publishers are doing the same thing as we do so that my comments should give you a pretty good feel about what publishers are up to. Basically, the Internet offered us a new form of marketing. We were able to aggregate our information into databases. In an era of increasing mergers, I am not sure how many independents are left. When you come to Penguin Putnam, you will find Viking Press, Berkeley, and other groups that we publish. We are aggregators in that area and try to help you find out about our multiple imprints.

Frontlists and backlists are both important. I really think the Web is a wonderful tool for supporting both areas. We are currently in the process of providing cover scans, reviews, and cataloging for our entire backlist. We hope to offer these features online in the near future. Another thing that we are trying to do is to reach the consumer and your patrons. One thing that interests me in the Web is that it isn't restrictive in any way. Access to our site is free to everyone all over the world. If you are interested in Jan Karon, you can come to our site. You can see where she is on tour and if she is coming to your community. You can learn many things about our authors. I think that this is a great service. In this way, we have done more to offer contact with us as publishers. We have offered subscription services that are free and the possibility of signing up to receive information about genres or authors that interest you. We have really had a great response to this new service. We have fifty thousand subscribers even though we have not been doing it that long.

The patrons and readers there are looking for information, and we are trying to provide it. The Internet is growing rapidly. We have felt it just as much as anyone else. We have a new site called Penguinclassics.com that I am going to use as an example of what we are trying to do to get away from the strictly marketing model that publishers used earlier and that accounts for most of the 41% that I gave at the beginning of my talk. As we go forward, we are trying to get more editorial comments on our Web sites. It is not enough just to provide online publisher catalogs. The catalogs work pretty well on the Web, especially for our backlist, but a Web site isn't great until you can find an essay—something that is original. We will also tell you about new and notable books, provide keyword searching, or let you know if there is a film tie in. We have hired staff who are dedicated to getting that information out on the Web for the reader and librarian. They are trying to make the Web site an educational as well as a marketing tool.

I think searching needs to mature. As an example from Penguinclassics.com, we support searching by author, title, ISBN, the original publication date, the region of origin, time period, and genre. For example, you can restrict your searches to West Indies poems of the seventeenth century. I believe that powerful searching can be helpful, particularly for librarians. Much of our subject classification is modeled after those used in libraries so that I think it will look familiar to you.

Discussion and community building are also important. Much of our traffic is from students, professors, academics, and general readers. They are all looking to discuss books. They are creating new topics every day. We have an editor who is dedicated to editing and moderating the discussion sessions. He is very busy. There are people every day who want to discuss specialized subjects such as Russian language. Professors come in who are teaching a class about Tolstoy and ask for suggestions. Besides being interesting, we have found it is a way to discover what people are reading. When you are publishing the classics, knowing your potential customers' reading habits is very useful information. We are trying to use the medium for more than just static marketing.

I think publishers will migrate toward this model as the Web speeds up and as we become more at ease with our place on the Web. We are trying to get original content on our site instead of just marketing content. We are putting up essays or reviews that have been written in the past or that are being written today. I should add that we include the complete review. These reviews do not say "terrific" in quotes as a *New York Times* advertisement would. It is good to read an essay on Russian literature that relates books to other books and that tells readers who are interested in Tolstoy that they might be interested in Pushkin. In fact, we have just brought out two more volumes on Pushkin.

As publishers add to their backlists, notifying readers about books in the way described earlier is a useful thing to do. It is not nearly so frontlist driven as when the backlist is tacked on at the end of information about recently published books. This allows for more of an organic experience in choosing books. Obviously, we have all the things that people have become accustomed to online. Making it easy to reach us is another key thing for us. I have heard people say that they can't get in touch with the publisher or that they can't get someone on the phone. This site allows us to receive e-mail and therefore provides more access to people who are at the other end of this process. I think the Web and e-mail are both wonderful media for that.

We have heard a lot of talk about the future today. With the aggregation of information and with everyone becoming an aggregator, the impetus should focus on users and what they need. When my parents heard I was becoming a bit of a Webhead, my father said: "Remember that a computer is a tool and you want it to do a job. If you want to build a house, you don't want to be the expert at using a hammer." That was an interesting comment. I think the Web is like that. In regard to the comments that I heard earlier about Amazon.com and about its customer reviews, I think we need to understand the Web and to realize that information may not always be completely reliable. It is definitely the case with publisher sites where we are interested in portraying our books in the best light. We are also providing essays and games on our site and are putting it all together to help librarians with book selection.

E-books and electronic monographs are important. I've been in the trenches with e-books for about six months. I've seen demos of every single product. They are coming; in fact, they are here. I have read a couple books on the Rocket E-book and SoftBook readers. They are quite impressive, and they are not going to go away. From a publisher's viewpoint, we see e-publishers as purveyors of the book experience. There are rights issues involved so that I think that we will move rather slowly. Leaps have been made, but it is not as if e-books are going to become a tidal wave. But this is something we need to be educated about, especially librarians. I have heard lots of talk about someone who downloads a book and then gives it to a friend to read. Is it my book, or is it my friend's? This is going to be an issue with circulation. Do you want them to take the device out of your library or the file? Do you buy a distributive file? This is going to be a tricky area in the future.

RICK AYRE

I'm Rick Ayre, vice president and executive editor at Amazon.com. When Jeff Bezos, chief executive officer and founder of Amazon.com, first hired me and gave me the title of vice president and executive editor, I was the seventieth employee. There are a few more people there now. He said that the title would impress publishers. We have made up a lot of titles as we have moved forward.

I meet often with business analysts in my duties as vice president. The business analysts often ask me: "What do you do as an editor at Amazon.com?" Today, I am grateful to be among people who understand what editors do and appreciate that effective communication is important. The good news is that, because the business people do not know what we do, we are very valuable to them because clearly they cannot do it themselves.

The other thing I should tell you about myself is that I like irony. I tell you this because, after I had an interview with the *Washington Post*, they said in the first page of the story that I loved postmodern ironic humor. Seeing it in print this way obviously makes it true. Therefore, I would like to start out with the king of postmodern ironic humor, Allan Greenspan: Greenspan, the Federal Reserve Board chairman, referring to an environment of international mergers, scurrying currency traders, and instantaneous Internet provided efficiency with which vast shifts of capital are decided and accomplished, acknowledged that the older order of slower change and more security, though less efficient, was more tranquil and less threatening to those with moderate or lesser skills. I am happy to be among a group with greater skills since this is one of the conclusions that I have made from your survey.

As we built Amazon.com, we tried to build a Web site that was exciting for people who could read. In fact, one of the advantages we had as we were building the site was that we were fairly certain that most of our users could read. That is not true for all the sites you find on the Web today. Many of you may have encountered the splashy graphics and the things that explode in your face and ears. At Amazon.com, we still try to communicate primarily with words. Someone who impressed me greatly with words is George W. S. Trow. He wrote a book a number of years ago *Within the Context of No Context*. He followed it up just recently with *My Pilgrim's Progress: Media Studies, 1950–1998*. Unfortunately, I can report that except for him so few of us have made any progress. He put forth the proposition that modern media, especially television, were destroying the context with which we interpreted events and that without this context there was a cultural void.

I would like to examine how we as a group might attempt to reverse that trend. Time does not move backward, but, as we move forward, we can perhaps influence the rise and fall of culture in the context of no context, at least in the areas of the library and cyberspace. "Computers are useless. They can only give you answers." Picasso said that. My mother was a librarian. I went to the library because I grew up in small town with no bookstore or movie theater. There was no Amazon.com back then.

When I visited the library, I used it in two ways. The first way was by searching. I knew the Dewey Decimal system by heart. I would go to the big boxes with cards in them and look up the books. That is the concept behind our original search page and still remains the concept behind our current search page. The way it worked when I started at Amazon.com was: author search—last name, first name, or initials. When, as a user, I was confronted with that page, I didn't know how to spell the whole name. Should I capitalize it? Does that matter? Can I go ahead and try if I know only part of the author's name? We kept these original instructions on the search page to show what searching used to be like in card catalogs or on the first version of our site. But today you can type in any part of an author's name or any part of the title. The subject search actually works. When users search, they are interested in results. When I did a keyword search for "Harris," those of you who love irony would appreciate that the first three results at the top of the page were the most likely responses for this search term. How do we know that? We have monitored the millions of people that have visited our site page and know which links most people visit first. We have used that aggregate data to rearrange our search results. Since we dynamically track searches, every twenty-four hours these results are rejiggered—that's our technical term for the process. When I did the search, the first three books in order were *Hannibal*, *Red Dragon*, and *Silence of the Lambs*. The next item, however, is *1st and 2nd Corinthians* because I must admit that, once you leave the boxes, the items are in alphabetical order. *Corinthians* unfortunately wasn't the next most popular.

The second way I used to search bookstores and libraries was to wander down the rows: first fiction and literature and then others. I would search the fiction section for authors alphabetically. At the literature and fiction page on our site, you can wander down those aisles as well.

The search page is very effective. We believe that the reason is partly because the people who create that page have a great passion for the content and also partly because they are helped by technology. You can search by an author's last name. You can search by categories. You can just wander down the aisles. According to your mood, you can search, or you can wander. But all this doesn't do any good unless we can convince people that they should be clicking. We cannot put everything on one page. They need to move between the pages, and, to do that, they have to click.

This is a big problem on the Web. How do you get people to click? It is a question of narrative strength—a well-known concept in my field. All you have to do is ride a commuter train to New York and watch how people fold their newspapers to know that newspapers have grappled with this problem for a long time. As you watch people fold newspapers, you know that sometimes they fold them correctly. Thus, narrative strength is something that has been an important part of our site. Here are some examples of narrative strength on our Web site. You can find what you are looking for on our site, but you should also be intrigued by something else. In the case above, for the people who bought a Harris book, there are lots of things to click, but it is now more than just a list of things to click on. It is the context surrounding those clicks that matters. You can navigate that site, but what intrigues you the most? I hope that the answer is narrative strength.

I looked at a picture that shows a Neil Young concert from the CD *Year of the Horse*. It is at the very beginning of the CD where he is moving from one song to the next. One fan shouts: "They all sound the same." Neil Young responds very quickly: "It's all one song." What you have here is the pragmatist talking to the philosopher. You have a detail person who hears a jangle of instruments, and you have Neil Young with the big picture view.

We have three home pages on our site. Though they might look the same, if you have that big picture view, we are creating a different context, in many important yet subtle ways, for each person who comes to the site. Each page caters to that individual. I put up a new user page that shows you that consumer shopping is guaranteed; the page then has editorial comment down the middle and includes features along the right-hand side like the "Hot 100 Books," which is updated every hour. One of my most respected colleagues thinks this is a great marketing trick.

We also have a video page. You can tell it's the video page because on the left side of the page is Tae Bo. This is the anchor on the video page because right now everyone in the world wants a copy of Tae Bo and who are we to get in the way of all those who want to buy it. Tae Bo will be there until everyone in the world has a copy or until the follow-up videos stop being produced. But along the middle of the page, the editors have time and space to create content. When you go to this page, you will find a lot more graphics on it than on the other pages. It turns out that the people who buy movies are visually attuned. They do not mind waiting for the pages to load.

We also have a music home page—again specifically designed for music lovers. It includes new and future releases, but another section, "artist essentials," is high on the page. "Artist essentials" is a new set of features created by the music people. It is a fantastic tool if you own artists like Bob Dylan or Bach and want to know the essential recordings that you need in your library.

Another way to create context online is to provide the same snapshot you see in the real world but with the depth that the online environment and the availability of databases allow you to add. The Web lets us give access to these databases. A list of award winners is nothing new since the book that won the Orange Prize would have been reported in many newspapers. One click below this, however, is all the books that were nominated for the prize and a list of previous prize winners. There are hot links to those books as well. In this way, we drive user interest and create context for all the award winners.

Best-sellers are a key topic. My favorite page is the *New York Times* best-seller list as it appears on our site. Our list is a little different than the *New York Times* because ours is sorted alphabetically. This change has legal consequences so that we are not sure how things are going to turn out. My favorite lawyer at Amazon.com is trying to do the right thing. Currently, we think the right thing to do is to fight the *New York Times* about its desire to make us remove our version. If we lose, we are willing to change it; but first we are going to fight for our version, much to the surprise of the people at the *New York Times* who initially said that we could rearrange it.

The other best-seller lists are updated every hour of every day. We also have daily best-seller lists that go a million deep. I like to track where my favorite books are on the best-seller list. Last time I looked, *Ulysses* was 768. This could only happen online. Because we celebrate books, we also celebrate the other places that celebrate books no matter where they appear in the media, even if the lists are from television or radio. I do not know about you, but when I read the newspaper every day, I have a hard time finding the book reviews. It is sometimes even difficult to find them in the *New York Times*. We gather all those reviews in one place. You can visit our site instead of trying to find a copy of *Entertainment Weekly*.

I would next like to make a few more general points. All of the kinds of things we do that make people think about books are things you can participate in with us. On the Web site from the Tacoma Public Library, you can look at their book catalog and see our logo. You can search about books there since the online system will tell you the information you want to know about the media type, which library branch has the book, and how many copies there are in the system. At the bottom of the page, it also says to check Amazon.com online bookstore for reviews and other information. Libraries can link to our site, no matter where the pages are located, if they want their users to have additional information including reviews and other facts about the book. The users can also buy it while they are there. If they do, the library that sent them to our site will get a commission from those sales. Regardless of what happens, this arrangement helps us.

Now a few words on truth and honesty. I know that reviews are a controversial topic. I have proof that it is controversial because the *New York Times* said on its front page that it is a controversial area. Our reviews are controversial because some people believe that reviews are bought and sold. Because I was coming to this particular convention and suspected that there would be some publishers in close proximity, I chose an example from our site. This is our review of Sheryl Crow's last album, *The Globe Sessions*. We sold lots of copies of this. It reads:

> For some fairly shallow performers, there comes a time when their craft becomes a chore, when scribbling songs for the big follow-up album turns into a black-and-white deadline. Clever composers can almost disguise this ennui, burying it in a smarmy, sunshine-beaming mix. Key word: *almost*. Ergo, a trial spin through clever composer Sheryl Crow's *The Globe Sessions* evokes the faintest hint of a feeling that grows stronger with each successive listening—there's no sense that the artist intended this material as anything more than tepid album filler.

And it goes on with a few more comments—most of them are not very complimentary. The review closes with: "If you support this silly sycophant with your hard-earned dollars, there's only one question that you'll need to be asked: Do you want paper or plastic?" This is an example of how the labels have purchased our reviews and how everything is bought and sold on our site.

There is nothing on our site that matters more to us than the information that we take great pride in providing to our users, whether they be librarians or book purchasers. We argue about objectivity all the time. I insist that our reviewers be honest and tell the truth as they see it. We build a book community by allowing the users to create their own context through their descriptions of the books. This is my favorite review on the site; it covers *The Tenth Justice* by Brad Meltzer, which was almost a best-seller a year ago.

> Imagine yourself in the following unfortunate predicament: you're stuck in the middle seat of a crowded airplane, in between two sweaty men of substantial girth, your flight starts doing one of those circling affairs three thousand feet from the airport due to bad weather, and the flight attendant announces that landing will not occur at any time in the foreseeable future. Then, perhaps, this would be a good book to pull out of your briefcase to read. Otherwise, be prepared to hit your head on the wall in absolute rage for having wasted a few hours of your life on a pretty poor piece of writing.

The complete review is still on the site if you want to read it.

Louis Pasteur used to exhort his students to make results seem inevitable. Of course, he was teaching them the scientific method that used independent and dependent variables so that his results were the results. But it is not that simple. Making results seem inevitable is an art form, but it is one we need to get pretty good at if we want to create context together. Since I like alliteration, content community cooperation creates context. I have used the word "context" somewhat tongue and cheek in this presentation regarding some of our Web context. But I am absolutely serious as an individual and as a company in saying that we struggle to give context for readers' lives. This is essential to our society and culture as we move forward. Therefore, together, I hope that we can get people excited and excite them to read and search for their own contexts. I believe that this is ultimately what we as publishers, vendors, and librarians need to achieve.

7

Buying from Publishers and Vendors

A Discussion among Librarians, Vendors, and Publishers Focusing on How Librarians Decide to Buy and from Whom

SARAH MICHALAK

I am here today as the chair of the Utah Academic Library Consortium. Our consortium has fifteen libraries and twelve institutions. Two years ago, the Utah legislature allocated directly to the library director council $1 million of base funding to distribute among the libraries in order to develop a new statewide model for collection development. The larger libraries in the consortium needed and wanted serials funding and money for databases. The smaller libraries wanted money for books. Our legislative liaison was very hesitant about going along with this idea because he felt that small libraries investing in their core book collections was not a new model and feared there would be a great deal of duplication. Nevertheless, we persevered. The large libraries argued with him as did the small libraries so that we ended up influencing him to accept our choice. The small libraries received additions of from 50% to 70% to their base budgets.

I want to talk to you about how the libraries have gone about spending that book money and about some of the observations we have made during the process. First, the small libraries from the very beginning wanted to establish approval programs and have done so. The reason is very simple since the smaller libraries are starved for staff; it is much less labor intensive to use an approval program instead of choosing individual titles through firm ordering.

One college librarian takes a purchase order in hand and travels the one hundred miles to Salt Lake City where she goes to Barnes and Noble and Borders to buy books. She usually takes along a faculty member. She usually brings the books back to the library and unpacks them in front of the students who are so starved for books that they flock around on unboxing day to look at what has been brought into the library. Her decision making is based solely on the titles that the faculty need to support their classes.

The Utah librarians developed an approach to improving statewide collections with the name "subject initiatives." In this approach, the consortium collection development committee selected six fields that are key areas for all the consortium members. They are science, education, nursing, criminal justice, fine arts, humanities, and audiovisual. The goal is to enhance the statewide collections and reduce duplication as much as possible. In criminal justice, for example, certain titles are appropriate for collections in community colleges. Other titles are more appropriate to serve graduate schools in social work or programs in sociology at research institutions. In nursing, our one state health science library collects the theoretical and research titles. The institution with vocational nursing programs selects more practical titles.

Initially, we envisioned that this program would spend a significant part of the funding on books. After two years of these projects, the pattern has developed to emphasize serials in both print and electronic full-text with lesser emphasis on books. The reason is that there has been some urgency in filling gaps in these high-profile disciplines. It takes a little bit longer to deal with all the individual decisions involved with buying books. In order to speed up acquiring titles without duplication to the individual institutions around the state, the librarians have tried a consortial approval program. We think that we are one of the first consortia around the country, except for OhioLINK, which has started a consortial approval program plan. As I said, criminal justice is the first subject we have worked on, and so far we are satisfied with the results. The nursing selectors took the core bibliography approach. They have used the Brandon Hill list to assign titles to the appropriate institutions within Utah.

I would like to think that the consortium market is valuable and should be attractive to publishers and vendors. We suggest that you study the needs of the end users like faculty and students, but especially faculty. That will help you determine the book buying patterns that you will see us pursue. You can help libraries explore ways to get books to users. Librarians want a faster turn around time since patrons are demanding quicker delivery from us. We are asking our vendors to help us satisfy our customers.

You might encourage libraries to use Amazon.com buying models for rush books and special requests. You will attract our business if you offer these services. Although the libraries in the consortium are reluctant to add new channels for acquiring books, we will do so if we can obtain these books at a faster pace. We will continue to favor the vendor approach. Vendors offer value-added services on which we now rely, such as interfacing with integrated library systems and so forth. These are all very important services that large and small institutions require. In an interesting development within the marketplace, we are experiencing a consolidation that has led to our using fewer vendors. Ordering through fewer vendors is less complicated and time consuming. Consortium buying will encourage this direction. Whole groups of libraries want to keep track of who is buying what with the result that we do not want to deal with lots of different vendors.

In some ways, our consortium follows trends depicted in the 1999 survey, but in other ways consortium collection development creates its own patterns and trends. In Utah, and I believe in other regions as well, the consortium environment is encouraging new trends, and old approaches are used in new situations. The larger libraries realized that, without the legislative testimonials of the smaller libraries, we would not have had the resources to continue to sustain our serials with the current high annual price increases. The smaller libraries realized that, without the ardent support of the research libraries, they would not have received the base support for book collections. We believe that consortia offer both vendors and publishers continued and, in some cases, increasingly fertile markets for books. Thank you for placing consortia among your most important customers.

KATHLEEN COTTER

I am from the Queens Borough Public Library. Our collection development program is a hybrid of centralized and decentralized collection development to serve the different purposes and plans we have in the library.

Central purchasing is, of course, the most efficient way to get materials quickly, inexpensively, and in massive quantities—which is what we like to do. We have a very high circulation, and we are working hard to keep it that way. Central purchasing is also a good way for us to buy electronic research resources. We generally put our electronic resources on the Queens Public Library home page so that our libraries have access to it regardless of their constituency and income level. Everyone using the Internet in one of the libraries has access to our materials on the Web. When we buy reference sources, we are looking at licensing the number of simultaneous users that we think will use the resource though that number varies from resource to resource. The other thing we always look for is remote access. Our customers who have access to the Internet at home like to dial up and use our resources.

One thing that we do in a decentralized way is to have books available in our book selection area for the branch librarians to come in to review for selection. Every two weeks, there is another set of books in that room. This option serves the purpose at Queens of empowering the library staff and of emphasizing the importance of the community library in Queens because Queens is an extremely diverse community. We have sixty-two branches, and each one varies in ethnicity, age distribution, and the kinds of materials that it is interested in. We want the branch librarians to be the ones that come in to choose books rather than having book selection done by those who sit in the central office.

We feel that we are well equipped to monitor the publishing industry for trends and to identify what the best-selling materials are going to be. The way we do that with my fairly small staff is through the traditional means of reviews. The backbone of our collection development selection is *LJ Alert*, the prepublication alert that comes out in every issue of *Library Journal*. It appears two to three months in advance of publication, a sufficient time for us to examine the individual titles. We also use vendor publications such as Baker and Taylor's *Booking Ahead* and Ingram's *Advance*. With those three resources as our core, we are able to identify the obvious future best-sellers. We also get some information about publicity, which is very important to us since it influences reader demand. We are then able to place our orders early to help get an advantageous discount from our vendors.

Another aspect of decentralized selection is to have the physical materials at hand, insomuch as possible, through approval plans and review copies so that the librarians can choose from the actual books in the selection room. Providing physical access is a trade-off because we sometimes get materials after publication since it takes time to get the materials organized and into the room. But we still find it is important to provide hands-on access for materials suitable for decentralized selection in contrast with the centralized materials that we try to identify and order early.

For centralized purchasing, we also spend a lot of time on Amazon.com. It's quick. It's fast. It shows a digitized image of the cover, which is really nice to see. We monitor its "Hot 100 Books." We often get requests from our branch customers for books that they have found on Amazon.com.

We also get information from the media. One thing we have found useful is the e-mail subscription service *PW Daily*—we read it every day. Before I left to come here, I read an article about *Layover* by Lisa Zeidner. *PW Daily* reviewed the book on the day that we were making our purchase decision. I think we were able to make a more informed decision than we would have otherwise made. I hope it will be a good decision.

I use a credit card for book purchases. I probably do not use it as extensively as I should, but I am getting more comfortable and familiar with the process. I tend to use a credit card on Amazon.com or BarnesandNoble.com for materials that I cannot get anywhere else. Otherwise, the lack of discount or the shipping charges make the price prohibitive for us. I also use the credit card in situations where we would otherwise have to prepay or when there is intense demand from in-house sources for a book to be purchased quickly.

We also work with many smaller vendors, jobbers, wholesalers, and a limited range of publishers. Some of those publishers' materials are hard to get through our review and approval plans and are hard to access in other ways. We get them to work with us or to send us approval copies of titles we have identified as interesting enough to consider purchasing. We do not do a lot of ordering from publishers, but we get a lot of information from them. We use the sites like the one for Penguin Putnam to get information. In general, we use the resources that the publishers provide.

The publishers that have marketing sales representatives are so helpful to us and give us so much information. They provide informative programs and study groups for us. We talk on the phone. They provide titles for us. We help them identify titles, and they help us identify titles. They are a really great resource for us, and I hope they will continue to operate as they presently do. The other thing that is important to us is their help in selling us materials, not only best-sellers, but books that we think are going to be sleepers or maybe reference books or nonfiction. We need to make sure that we get copies out to all the branches. We generally buy those materials from major vendors. My goal is to maintain a variety of vendors and to split the orders evenly among the major vendors to keep a balance. We use vendors for the same reasons that you have already heard today—because of the processing and outsourcing services they provide.

My processing staff was created at a time when we spent $1 million annually on books, but we now spend about $10 million a year on books. We still have the same staff in the same rooms using basically the same equipment. The increased volume has overwhelmed the people in those positions so that I have outsourced processing for best-selling materials, especially fiction. Outsourcing is probably going to get more extensive as we go further along this road because we plan to send more materials to them.

We look for various things in selecting a vendor. Of course, discount is important. We know that there are some areas and titles that vendors and publishers like more than others, and we try to track that. The level of service is important. Our relationship with the sales representatives of larger and smaller vendors is good. With other people in these organizations, the service can vary. Some are very helpful so that, when my clerks are trying to track down a title, it is easy. Some vendors are not as easy to deal with. We have to call the 1-800 number and take what we get. If I know I may have to track things down later, it will affect the decision about where I make the first purchase.

We also consider the value-added services that vendors provide such as processing and cataloging. The book lists that they can provide when we are doing special projects are also important. The library marketing survey has been helpful in letting me compare what we do with practices in other libraries. I cannot emphasize enough how important that has been. For those of us who work for city agencies and quasi-agencies, we must prove accountability and show to our city council and mayor what we are doing and how productive we are. For those purposes, these types of statistics are very important. When people talk about what they want from publishers and vendors, any statistics that can be added to those that we get from our circulation and acquisition system would be most helpful.

REBECCA JAMES

I am the individual from the vendor community that has been asked to comment on the survey. I am going to do so in a couple of ways. I am going to comment directly on survey respondents and what they said. Then I am going to comment from my fifteen years' experience as a vendor and as a librarian about what I am personally seeing and experiencing. I want to tell you that, from the vendor perspective, the libraries I deal with differ percentage-wise from the respondents in the survey. Eighty percent of the customers I work with are public libraries as opposed to the survey respondents who are 35% public libraries. Keep this in mind as you listen to my comments.

On the vendor side, at least 60% of our orders are received electronically, and this number is growing. The survey said that 34% of respondents use electronic methods of ordering. Everything I looked at in the survey regarding electronic methods was much lower than is the case with the libraries I work with. My comments will reflect that. If 60% of our orders are coming electronically, than 40% are coming from manual methods that include mail, fax, and phone. The survey had 65.6% manual ordering. Thus, the numbers are reversed in my experience.

I am going to comment on a few important vendor promotional methods, the most useful types of mailings from vendors and publishers, the most frequently used sources for book selections, the effectiveness of review sources for library sales, and the top factors used in making executive decisions. I will also comment very briefly on backlist purchases.

We have heard over and over again today that reviews are still important for libraries. They were important back when I went to library school twenty years ago, and reviews still seem to be the number one factor in selection. Catalogs also are high on the list of effective promotional methods from vendors and publishers. It was a confirmation to me when I saw the statistics that show the efforts vendors take to make available review citations and full-text reviews for print and electronic materials. I was pleased to learn that these efforts are well worth our time. If vendors are not providing this service, they should take a closer look at doing so. Publishers should also consider this since it is a key issue.

State library shows, not national shows, are high on the list of good promotional methods. Furthermore, direct mail was given high grades for usefulness. Telemarketing was one of the methods people do not like. It was not seen as a useful practice though I know of some publishers who have used telemarketing effectively, not to sell titles, but to give information about new titles. I think there is some real value in this type of telemarketing.

National conferences like those of the American Library Association and the American Booksellers Association were not thought of as being important for promotion. I cannot imagine that we as a company are going to stop going to conferences whether they be state, regional, or national. The amount of booth traffic and the number of people coming to find out about products and services justify our presence. I am not sure why respondents did not feel that conferences were important. It may reflect the type of people who responded and the types of budgets they have for going to conferences. If you cannot afford to go, you are not likely to consider conference attendance as a useful source of information.

Sales calls were also considered as not very important. This is directly opposed to my experience. Someone also alluded to the fact that your sales representative is an important person in helping you deal with many issues. I think sales representatives will continue to be supported in the field.

Next, I want to talk about the most useful mailings from vendors and publishers. The survey respondents listed things like subject catalogs, complete catalogs, forthcoming announcements, fliers, and selection ordering tools. They all rate as fair and many rate high in usefulness in the survey responses from vendors and publishers. Since libraries use this information, many vendors and publishers have made these mailings into a valuable resource. What I am being asked for more and more is whether this information is available in electronic formats, even if on a disk, rather than on paper. Many customers also ask for a way to FTP this information. Libraries are able to use electronic products in many creative ways. They can take information in an electronic file and then slice and dice it to make it more useful to their libraries. They can personalize and customize it to meet their needs. Personally, I think we are going to see a lot more information in electronic formats.

According to the survey, the most frequently used types of information for book selection purposes were library reviews, media reviews, publishers' catalogs, vendor selection tools, general book trade reviews, such as *Publishers Weekly*, and newspaper book reviews, such as the *New York Times*. I was surprised that bibliographic tools, such as *Books in Print* and *Vendor Database*, were not found as useful by these survey respondents. This surprised me because there are a number of comprehensive databases available today in electronic formats that have full-text reviews associated with them or at least have citations to reviews. Since reviews are important, I would have thought that databases, that often include reviews, would be important as well. The company that I work with has thousands of libraries using our Web-based selection tools as a very important part of their selection process.

The effectiveness of publications as review sources amused me. As I mentioned, I went to library school over twenty years ago, but the important review sources have not changed at all. Publications like *Library Journal, Booklist, Choice, School Library Journal, Publishers Weekly*, and *New York Times Book Review* received very effective ratings. Vendor publications were used but to a lesser extent. Web sites like Amazon.com and BarnesandNoble.com are getting increased attention. Top factors used in making purchasing decisions have not changed in twenty years—content reviews, reputation of author, reputation of publishers, and award winner lists.

Discounts are still the number one factor with libraries for vendor selection, but vendor service levels are also mentioned as being important. I am happy to see that libraries are realizing that there is a price tag associated with service and that discounts are not the only determinant. There are many factors going into the equations of what works best, including economically, for the library.

I noticed that, according to survey respondents, libraries are not spending much money on backlist purchases. I am very excited about on-demand printing as a way to keep titles in print forever and to develop better rounded collections.

NANCY PEARL

The Seattle Public Library has a major research library, which we call our central library, and twenty-three branches. It is administratively a department of the City of Seattle. This means that the Seattle Public Library is a huge bureaucracy. What we have found out is that it is much easier to order from and pay one invoice than to order from and pay many different invoices.

We probably order between 85% to 100% of our books from vendors. We choose our vendors on factors beyond discount because discounts tend to be very similar. Our factors in choosing vendors include their helpfulness and the willingness of their sales representatives to work with us. We do find, as Peter McCallion said, that we use vendor sales representatives for troubleshooting. On the other hand, it does not make a lot of sense for publisher sales representatives to call on us for routine visits because we do not have time for them. When I managed an independent bookstore, we welcomed sales representatives, sat down, and went over the catalog. We consider many of the same things in making selections in the library, but we simply do not have the time to spend listening to someone present the fall list.

It makes more sense for us to make our selections by reading the review media and to base our purchasing decisions on these recommendations. We do not have approval plans. We find that we really need to handle twenty-five to one hundred copies of the book at one time and have them cataloged together and sent out together to all the branches. Even gifts, which you would think we would love, interrupt the flow of getting the materials out to the customers who are waiting for them.

The most important thing I would say to you as publishers is that you need to find out who in the library is responsible for making the selection decision, not necessarily who does the ordering because that is often a different department. It just breaks my heart when I look at the number of catalogs that come in and are sent to people who have nothing to do with the selection process. It is really important to make it your business to find out if a library has centralized ordering. In this case, the only important person that you want to get that catalog to is the person who is doing the centralized buying in that particular area. On the other hand, if the system has individual ordering from the branch libraries, then it makes sense to send out catalogs. But often sending out hundreds of catalogs is a waste of time, money, and trees.

Another very important factor for publishers to think of when it comes to libraries is to have someone in your company who is interested in libraries and is responsible for marketing to them. Having someone like Marci Purcell from Random House or Virginia Stanley from HarperCollins makes all the difference in the world. Having them come to conferences like BookExpo America and show some semblance of interest in the library market means a lot to us as librarians.

YVETTE BERTHEL DIVEN

I would like to focus on three areas that were addressed by both the 1986 and the 1998 surveys:

1. The growth of budgets for electronic resources.
2. The influence of nonlibrary personnel on the decision-making process.
3. The decision about whether to buy through vendors or buy direct from publishers for electronic resources.

In 1986, the same year that *Books in Print PLUS* on CD–ROM was launched, only 10% of library respondents expected their budgets for electronic databases to increase during the next five years. Among the publisher respondents, however, an overwhelming majority (some 80%) expected libraries to increase their budgets for electronic resources. (Publishers were a very hopeful group!)

The most recent survey reveals the trend toward larger budgets for electronic resources, specifically remote-access databases and other online resources. At Bowker, we have seen this trend in all segments of the library market, with the biggest growth among libraries participating in statewide initiatives and particularly among those libraries that are mandated to bring online access and online databases to their K–12 schools. This often means bypassing the CD–ROM option and moving directly from print to remote online databases.

"How Libraries Decide to Buy and from Whom" is also influenced by nonlibrary personnel. This is especially true in the academic market, among college and university libraries, and for schools offering distance learning programs. In 1986, librarians in college and university environments identified faculty and other nonlibrary personnel as influential in identifying new library print resources. The latest survey echoes this. With budgets growing for electronic resources, we might suggest that a future trend will be the greater influence of faculty members on the identification and recommendation of electronic resources. The desire for remote access from faculty offices, as well as students' dorms and the desktops of distance learners, will continue to drive this trend.

Increased spending on electronic resources will change the role of the publisher in the library's purchasing decision. The 1986 survey suggested that libraries of all types spent 60% of their budgets with vendors. In the new survey, that number is even higher. As libraries purchase more electronic resources—namely, remote-access databases—publishers' roles will be expanded. More and more publishers will themselves become vendors and will sell their electronic resources directly to libraries. Certainly, the content of electronic resources and reviews of those resources will continue to be important factors in the selection and purchasing process. But publishers will be held to a higher standard than just having a good database. The same factors that the survey tells us influence libraries' selection of book vendors—customer service and troubleshooting as well as a good price—will have a great influence on their decisions about selecting publishers for direct purchases. In addition, publishers who partner with vendors—whether library automation vendors or database access providers—will be the most successful in getting libraries' business. To recap, we can say that:

- Libraries will be spending more on electronic resources, especially remote-access databases.
- Identification of which electronic resources are valuable to library users will increasingly come from outside the library.
- Decisions to buy these online resources direct from publishers will be influenced by many of the same criteria used to select vendors for print materials.
- Publishers who partner with vendors to offer libraries more choices in accessing publishers' electronic resources will be more successful than those who choose to go it alone.

PETER MCCALLION

I am the acquisitions person on this panel to talk about how we decide to buy books. I was quite surprised this morning at the proportion of people who filled out the survey since a majority had not. I was a member of the survey team in 1975 and spoke on the panel. At that time, I remember that we were discussing with the publishers and vendors a practice that the librarians were diametrically opposed to. This big issue was telemarketing, which the publishers and wholesalers thought was wonderful. The librarians told them exactly what we thought of it. Things are still much the same today.

As I was looking at the buying part of the survey, one thing jumped out at me that was so strange that I hope it is just how the questionnaire was answered rather than reality—the findings on the role of the sales force and the sales representative. I would like to echo and agree with Rebecca James that the quality of the sales force and the sales representative is one of the most important factors I use in deciding where to buy a book. When I had a really good sales representative who left one company for another, quite often, if the new company was a wholesaler with the same type of material, I would transfer my business. All things being equal, my sales representative knew what I wanted. By knowing her job, she made my job a little easier.

I will talk today a bit more about sales forces and sales representatives though I worry that I am preaching to the converted. I would like to give a couple of the statistics from the questionnaire and survey responses. I was shocked when I read that 65% of libraries say no to sales calls, sales representatives, and sales forces. It is unbelievable to me that they would do so. It is such an important point. To quote a famous movie: "The force is with us." Eighty percent of the wholesalers' budgets for library marketing and library sales are spent on their sales forces. They are obviously doing this because they expect something positive to happen with the money they are spending. Yet only about 6% of the library respondents felt the sales force or the representative was the most important or one of the most important factors in considering where to purchase a book. Since so many things are equal, I found this bit of information surprising.

When talking about publishers' representatives, 6% thought they were useful in learning about the library market, publishing trends, and marketing trends. For the wholesalers, it was higher at 13% to 14% who felt they were getting important information from these representatives. How are we going to know what is coming out and how to save money for books or what is going to happen in the market for paperback versus large print versus hardcover versus recorded materials if we don't know and talk to these people to find out about marketing trends?

One of the questions on the survey was: "What do you think is the main responsibility of your service representative when he or she comes to make a call for you?" Fifty percent expect publisher representatives to troubleshoot problems, and 20% expected them to talk about trends in research. For the vendor representatives, the numbers were higher. They said 70% of the calls were troubleshooting, and 20% were on marketing and developments in the industry. There is the problem. If only 5% of the publishers felt that troubleshooting was the main reason to have a sales call, maybe they were not selling directly to the libraries. I cannot imagine that, if you are buying directly from a publisher, only 5% of the calls dealt with problems. I think that is why wholesalers are doing so well these days because publishers are doing such a bad job in shipping and handling that we let wholesalers handle the problems. We let them fight about reordering so that, when we get a book, it comes in complete and we can just pay the invoice.

From their responses, 92% of the vendors felt that troubleshooting was the most important reason for the visit. But 41% felt that talking to librarians about trends they saw happening in marketing to libraries was very important. Twenty-five percent felt that sharing publishing and marketing information was important.

I guess I would like to find out what makes a good sales representative. What would I like to get from a sales representative instead of a nice lunch, a chance to get out of the building to get a cup of coffee, or an opportunity to get away from my desk? I would like a representative to be truthful. I would like him to respond to my questions and to tell me about the status of orders and the availability of materials. If there is a problem, would I like to go to him to get the invoice corrected. The representative can tell me what happened to the missing shipment or take care of the problem of my being asked to pay for something that never arrived or for something that I returned as damaged when the company claims that it wasn't.

The other thing I would like during the sales call is for the sales representative to tell me that in six or seven months his company is going to install a new computer system or that in two months it will change software. That tells me to watch my orders and my invoices more carefully. I should call in a week if I do not get a response in case the system crashed. I might be getting duplicate bills, extra charges, duplicate shipments, or shipments to the wrong library. Knowing about changes ahead of time will make my life a little bit easier. I would know that my money is well spent with this company. Most importantly, I would like to know when the warehouse will be closed for inventory or empty for whatever reason. This is a very important piece of information with the large budget that I have to spend because I need to know from whom to order. If Wholesaler A is slowing down in August, I would go to Wholesaler B for orders during that period because I know I would get a better fill rate.

I would hope that the representative would come to see me two or three times a year. I would hope he would call me if there were any important information for me. I would also like to have him return my calls quickly if I leave a telephone message. If I deal with a company without a representative, I would like to talk to the same person in customer service every time I call. I hope that the librarians in the audience have a good working relationship with their representatives and that the publishers and vendors have a very good relationship with their libraries because that is one of the most important things I consider when placing book orders.

8

Conclusions

EUGENIE PRIME AND PATRICIA SCHROEDER

EUGENIE PRIME

Two quotations came to mind as I sat here during the proceedings. One of them is by Benjamin Disraeli, who was prime minister of Great Britain in the nineteenth century. He allegedly said: "There are three kinds of lies: lies, damned lies, and statistics." Artemus Ward said: "It's not what you don't know that can get you into trouble, but it's what you know that ain't so." These things went through my mind today. As one speaker pointed out, a survey is a snapshot in time. We have to remember this. It is what happens after the survey that is important because the future is where we will all be working and living. Thus, what happens after we leave this room is what is going to be critically important.

Another thing is that from 1977–1979 is two years, and 1987–1989 is two years. The three years—1997, 1998, and 1999—are a lifetime. The big difference is the Internet. Everything that happens is happening at a faster pace than it happened before. Second, everything happens discontinuously. This is the time of change. There are changes that have blindsided us. At the time of the last survey, could you have predicted the Web or Amazon.com? The point I am making is the need to examine the attitude that we have toward change, the openness we have to change, and our willingness to embrace or to not embrace technology and change. I wish there were some way that the surveys could capture qualitative issues and not just quantitative ones. The numbers mean absolutely nothing by themselves. Thankfully, we had people today who could interpret the numbers and make them come alive.

What do I have to say? I have one important point. The future does not just happen. We create the future by what we do and fail to do. We have what people call a triangle. We have enough people in this room to help create the future. Are we going to wait another twelve years to have a survey? Are we going to wait another twelve years to have a discussion like this between three important groups? If we do wait, in twelve years I don't know who will be sitting in a place like this. I don't know who the players will be. So we can't wait that long.

There was a piece of the program where, like Francine Fialkoff, I wanted to get on my soapbox. The hardest thing for me to do was sit in my seat while Francine talked about how 56% of publishers do not have a coordinator for library services. I sat back there and said: "What is $3.5 billion? What are we, chopped liver? Are we not important?" How can you find out how to serve us best if you don't have anybody important enough to be a coordinator?

I realized why there was this disconnect. Librarians know what marketing means. The publishers and vendors here were talking about selling and promoting. There is a difference. As Peter Drucker said: "Marketing is the philosophical alternative to force." At my library we have a full-time marketer, yet publishers don't have a full-time marketer for the library market. There are a number of people who talked about disconnects, and this is one of them.

Linked to that point was the issue of exhibits. Somebody talked about the concern that exhibits were not important to the library market. Somebody refined it by saying exhibits are not effective as a promotional vehicle. This is particularly disturbing. I think exhibits are a marketing tool. I see exhibits as the second most important reason I attend a convention. Networking is first, and exhibits are second. They give me an idea of the trends and let me know what is happening in the field. Most of all, it is a time to talk to publishers and to complain. Where else am I going to get you as a captive audience to listen to me?

At lunch time, I went to Netlibrary.com. Where else could I tell them that it is a stupid idea for me to borrow a book for two weeks and then to have it self-destruct? Where else could I tell them that the idea of buying ten titles in an age of electronic distribution does not make sense. Why can't I buy one title with ten simultaneous users? The neat part of what they said back to me is that libraries are on the cutting edge and that it is the publishers who are holding back everything.

The other point that to me was extremely important was that word called "service." I didn't hear enough of that word today. I liked that Martha Whittaker said that she doesn't sell books but instead all the services that wrap around the book. This is a very important and very smart statement. Unfortunately, that statement was followed up by her saying that service is what differentiates vendors and that they are giving it away. You are not giving it away. You just said you are not selling the books. We are buying what you sell around the books. How could you be giving it away? If you think you're giving it away, try to take it away, and see how many books you sell. The worst thing to do is to get someone accustomed to something and then tell them that you are going to price it or take it away. To me, these services have become our inalienable right. What do you mean you are going to take it away? Service is everything. Stanley M. Davis and Christopher Meyer wrote a book called *BLUR: The Speed of Change in the Connected Economy* in which they talked about the fact that products are becoming more like services. Let me say to the vendors and publishers out in the audience: "Service is everything."

People talked about e-books. There are e-books, and then there are e-books. I'm no Luddite, but let us look at e-books. When you look at them, not all e-books lend themselves to being e-books. I cannot imagine curling up on a winter day, as much of a winter day as we have in California, at the fireplace with an e-book. But there are certain materials that do lend themselves to electronic formats much better. Reference titles and handbooks, for example, are useful when you need discrete bits of information. They are books that you want to pop in and out for information. They are not the sort of thing that you will sit and read right through. An adequate resolution for e-books is not yet available. From working with a company that deals with resolution, I believe that the resolution is not going to be there for quite sometime.

Tony Ferguson made a point this morning that was very true. He said: "Students want information, and formats will increasingly become less important." The person from Penguin noted that information is just two clicks away. The number of clicks that you are away from the information is important. It is not enough to say that I have a Web site. Important for the Web site is the user interface, and important for the interface is how fast I can get to the information I need. Ten clicks away is as far as walking to your library.

In the relationship between vendors and publishers as we move more into the electronic age, one person raised the critical point about the role of vendors, particularly at this point where electronic information is so fluid. When I buy a book, I know it will cost $10.95. I know that this is the average price; I feel great if I can get it for $9.95 or even $10.49. With electronic information, the price you pay is what you negotiate for. There are many people who are not willing to give that negotiation power over to a third party. There is so much that is fluid in that area that I think we are in a situation where we are doing a little ballet dancing as we decide what the role of the vendor will be in the electronic database marketplace. I think we will find future developments to be very interesting.

Another trend that will be interesting to watch is on-demand printing. We are moving from the time when you print it and distribute it to a time when you distribute information about availability and print as needed. How does that change things? One thing that concerns me as a user is the fact that I have heard publishers talk about selling direct from the wonderful Web sites that they have created. I want to leave this one thought with you as the biggest concern because it creates a multiplicity of proprietary gateways to get information. Where is this going to end? It creates a heavy burden on users. You are asking them to learn a lot more than I believe they are willing to learn.

As a passing comment, publishers have a wonderful opportunity to shape and change e-commerce. One of the things you could start doing, without worrying about antitrust violations, is standardizing at least the terms on your Web site so that when I see "search" it means "search" regardless of the Web site I'm in and that the word "order" means the same thing for every site. In addition, you could create standardized icons. For example, everyone knows the meaning of an icon with a red line through it. Forget the cutesy to give me something that I can understand and relate to. We all have the opportunity to shape the future; let's live up to the challenge.

PATRICIA SCHROEDER

I think we have all come to the conclusion that we don't need a Polaroid shot once every ten years. When you take a Polaroid picture, it is a very accurate view of what you happen to be looking at, but the market is so much broader. There are many more things to see. If there is anything we are all sure of, it is how dynamic everything is. The other thing we can never forget, that I think is so terribly important, is that we are really looking at the people we are trying to get this content to. We never want to leave them out of the equation. I think it is getting much harder because people at home have all these resources called My AOL or My Yahoo. They can channel themselves into a hole and never find out what is going on in the broader world.

I think what libraries are doing by providing a much broader scope, by being in the community, and by trying to pull people up and out of My Yahoo to a larger view is more critical than ever. We cannot forget that. The book has got to be at the library when the patron comes in and asks for it, or he or she might not come a second time. We never want to forget who the end user is. That is why I worry a little bit about the image of a triangle as we talk to each other without paying enough attention to why we do it all—to reach the end user.

One of the suggestions that Nora Rawlinson made was that we need more librarians at BookExpo America (BEA), and that we need more publishers at the American Library Association Conference. We really need to come to each other's conventions instead of waiting another ten years for a Polaroid shot that prompts us to sit down to talk to each other. I think that coming to the conventions is a very good way to find out what publishers are talking about because they are all over the exhibit floor and have displays. Some time ago, publishers felt a little intimidated about coming to ALA because, for a while, technology displays dominated the exhibit and everyone was into the whiz-bang look. I think publishers felt that they weren't as front and center as they had been in the past. I hope that we can work this problem out to make people feel comfortable everywhere. I think librarians don't go to BEA because they feel it is more geared to booksellers. So let us figure out how to sponsor forums at both of these events where we can have more dialogue because I think talking to each other is terribly important.

I particularly liked the comments on pricing, probably because women like shopping. I remember that, when I was growing up, there were some people who knew the price of everything and the value of nothing. Now I know the price of nothing, and I'm not sure I know the value of anything either. I think that is because it is no longer content that is priced anymore. Look at cars. Look at your hotel room. You know everyone in the hotel paid a different price for his or her room. I never ask anyone on an airline about what they paid for their ticket because I always end up being the one that paid the most. I think society is totally frustrated at this moment with pricing because we all want to get value, but it is so complex to do so. How do you figure things out? We want to make sure that the vendors' goal isn't to keep everything too complex for us to figure it out because otherwise we might want to price shop. How do we bring all that together?

My kids are a lot better at doing this than I am. They will get on the Internet. I don't think there is anything that I have bought that they haven't bought at a cheaper price. They look at me like a real dodo. But I don't want to spend twenty hours on the Net—I've got a life. I'm sure librarians feel a little bit that way. I think that as publishers discuss how they can deal more directly with you through their Web sites they ought to have this kind of input. What makes it easier? When will you take time to access it? When will you say just forget it and go to some place that you know?

We know that, whatever happens, this market will continue to change. If we wait another ten years, we will look quite silly. In the meanwhile, we really, really need to work together to get people to read and to make sure they understand how exciting reading is. We have some of these "Get Caught Reading" promotional materials on the floor; I'm wearing the same colors as you can tell. We had good results from that promotion, and we would like to work with librarians wherever we can to get people excited about reading. I think for so very long every other industry was out there telling people that really "cool" people don't read, or that "cool" people wear headphones, buy DVDs, or immerse themselves in a whole range of other activities.

If there is any place on the planet that you want to know about, you can get wonderful authors with incredible insights. It is just amazing in this global world that we live in that reaching out is more important than ever. While we should be learning more about the broader world, technology is allowing some people to retreat into their "holes" so that people who listen to Dr. Laura only talk to people who like Dr. Laura. I can see our jobs becoming more imperative than ever to get a broad range of information out. We need to get people excited about the wider world so that they want to access it. Let's figure out how to overcome all these little glitches that keep us from moving forward. Let's keep the dialogue going.

If you come to BEA, I promise you that AAP will set up some forums where we can have real dialogue. If you like this idea, tell us, and we will do it. We hope that we can get publishers saying that it was informational. We will come to ALA and continue this back-and-forth dialogue in smaller groups where you can talk about specifics. I think that this dialogue can be really helpful for all of us because these are internal housekeeping hurdles. Our real goal is to discover how to break outside. We need to shut down the circle and the blame game to find out what we can do together. We need to get on with pushing reading as exciting and move forward. If you will come to BEA, I promise you that we will have publishers there. Let's not wait ten years to do this again.

II

Results of the AAP/ALCTS Library Marketing Survey

9

AAP/ALCTS Library Marketing Survey Publisher Questionnaire: Summary of Survey Responses (N = 77)

1. Which one of the following best describes your company? (CIRCLE ALL THAT APPLY.)

Trade publisher	50.6%
Children's publisher	31.2%
Reference publisher	31.2%
Professional/technical publisher	33.8%
Audio publisher	9.1%
Electronic/online publisher	14.3%
Other See "Other Responses" List for Q.1	26.0%
Base:	77

2a. About how many new book titles does your company publish annually? (CIRCLE THE NUMBER OF THE ANSWER.)

Under 100	50.6%
100 to 300	31.2%
301 to 500	5.2%
Over 500	13.0%
Total:	100.0%
Base:	77

b. How many new multimedia titles do you publish annually?

Under 10	89.2%
10 to 50	6.2%

51 to 100	1.5%
Over 100	3.1%
Total:	100.0%
Base:	65

3a. About how many book titles do you currently have in print altogether?

Under 100	6.7%
100 to 300	14.4%
301 to 500	9.2%
501 to 800	17.1%
801 to 1,000	10.5%
1,001 to 5,000	27.6%
5,001 to 10,000	6.7%
Over 10,000	7.8%
Total:	100.0%
Base:	76

b. How many multimedia titles do you currently have in print altogether?

Under 10	77.3%
10 to 50	15.2%
51 to 100	3.0%
Over 100	4.5%
Total:	100.0%
Base:	66

4. Currently, what are the annual sales of your company in the USA via all channels?

Under $1 million	12.7%
$1 million to $10 million	59.2%
$11 million to $70 million	21.1%
$71 million to $100 million	0.0%
Over $100 million	7.0%
Total:	100.0%
Base:	71

5. What percentage of your company's current total sales are to libraries?

1 to 10 percent		30.7%
11 to 20 percent		21.3%
21 to 40 percent		13.3%
41 to 60 percent		12.0%
Over 60 percent		<u>22.7%</u>
	Total:	100.0%
	Base:	75

6a. What percentage of your total sales to libraries comes in via distributors or vendors?

1 to 10 percent		17.1%
11 to 20 percent		7.9%
21 to 40 percent		5.3%
41 to 60 percent		17.1%
61 to 80 percent		22.4%
Over 80 percent		<u>30.2%</u>
	Total:	100.0%
	Base:	76

b. Would you like to see this segment of your sales mix . . .

Increase,		47.3%
Decrease, or		20.3%
Remain about the same?		<u>32.4%</u>
	Total:	100.0%
	Base:	74

7a. What percentage of your total sales to libraries is direct business?

1 to 10 percent		41.3%
11 to 20 percent		22.7%
21 to 40 percent		12.0%
41 to 60 percent		8.0%
61 to 80 percent		6.7%
Over 80 percent		<u>9.3%</u>
	Total:	100.0%
	Base:	75

b. Would you like to see this segment of your sales mix:

Increase	66.2%
Decrease	2.7%
Remain about the same	31.1%
Total:	100.0%
Base:	74

8a. What percentage of your company's overall marketing expenditure is directed at library markets?

None	(SKIP TO Q.9a)	9.2%
1 to 10 percent		28.9%
11 to 20 percent		25.0%
21 to 50 percent		7.9%
51 to 70 percent		7.9%
71 to 90 percent		7.9%
Over 90 percent		13.2%
	Total:	100.0%
	Base:	76

b. What percentage of your library marketing budget is spent in the following categories? (IF UNSURE, GIVE YOUR BEST ESTIMATE.)

Direct mail	26.1%
Telemarketing	2.8%
Sales representatives	5.6%
Catalogs	26.9%
Publicity	1.7%
Space advertising	12.4%
Exhibits:	
State	2.5%
Regional	0.5%
National	12.4%
Flyers	4.4%
Newsletters	0.7%
Web site	2.7%
Other	1.3%
Total:	100.0%
Base:	63

9a. Is there a person, or persons, in your company whose primary responsibility is marketing to libraries?

Yes		44.0%
No	(SKIP TO Q.10)	56.0%
	Total:	100.0%
	Base:	75

b. Indicate the title(s) of the person(s) who have this responsibility:
1. President
2. Sales Manager
3. Publisher and Special Sales Manager
4. School Library Sales Manager
5. Library Marketing Manager
6. Dir. of Development, Marketing Manager
7. Manager of Sales and Promotion
8. VP Library Sales
9. Account Representatives
10. Marketing Director
11. Library Marketing and Sales Director
12. Special Sales
13. Library Marketing Director
14. Director of Marketing
15. Promotions Coordinator
16. Library and Education Marketing Director
17. Director of Marketing
18. Marketing Manager, Wholesale Liaison Coordinator
19. Associate Marketing Manager
20. Library and Corporate Sales
21. Director of Library Promotion
22. Journals Marketing Coordinator
23. VP Marketing, Marketing Mgr/WHLSE/Ch. Bks, Mgr. Direct
24. Managing Editor
25. Library Relations Mgr.
26. Dir. of Academic/Lib. Mkt., Institutional Sales
27. Chairman
28. Marketing Manager

29. Marketing Director
30. Dir. of Adult Academic Library Marketing, Dir. of School Library Marketing

10. How important do you think each of the following are to librarians in deciding to buy from a publisher? (RATE EACH ON A SCALE FROM 1 = "Very important" TO 5 = "Not at all important.")

	Very Important				Not at All Important
Price	16.0%	30.7%	37.3%	16.0%	0.0%
Discount	17.8	30.1	31.5	15.1	5.5
Reviews	55.8	31.2	11.7	0.0	1.3
Reputation of author	22.1	46.7	23.4	6.5	1.3
Inclusion on recommended lists and awards	40.1	37.3	13.3	8.0	1.3
Media coverage	6.8	28.8	37.1	20.5	6.8
Web site, online publicity, and information	5.5	13.7	35.6	32.9	12.3
Author tours	2.7	12.3	23.3	37.0	24.7
Binding quality	13.2	43.4	30.3	11.8	1.3
Binding type	9.2	38.2	40.8	11.8	0.0
Acid free paper	14.3	28.6	38.9	11.7	6.5
Bibliographic tools like CIP, BIP	33.3	36.0	22.7	6.7	1.3
Overall reputation of publisher or imprint	29.9	45.4	18.2	5.2	1.3
Content	56.0	40.0	4.0	0.0	0.0
Free freight	4.1	16.2	40.5	28.4	10.8
Customer service	14.3	31.2	46.7	6.5	1.3

On-time shipping with adequate packing standards	20.8	33.7	32.5	13.0	0.0
EDI capability	5.5	5.5	38.3	37.0	13.7
Toll-free 800 order numbers	10.5	15.8	44.7	23.7	5.3
Telemarketing	3.9	3.9	11.7	49.3	31.2
Sales representatives	2.6	13.0	29.9	37.6	16.9
Availability of standing orders	7.8	23.4	45.4	20.8	2.6
Preprocessing services	12.2	25.7	33.7	24.3	4.1
Promotional materials	7.9	25.0	42.1	21.1	3.9
Direct mail	14.3	27.3	37.6	15.6	5.2

<---- Row percents sum to 100.0% ---->
(Average Base = 75)

11. How do you see the library market changing over the next five years for these kinds of publications:

	Substantial Increase	Some Increase	Some Decrease	Substantial Decrease	No Change
Hardcover adult	6.3%	45.3%	28.1%	7.8%	12.5%
Paperback adult	11.1	73.0	1.6	3.2	11.1
Hardcover children	4.9	50.8	26.2	3.3	14.8
Paperback children	13.6	59.2	13.6	1.7	11.9
Reference	12.1	37.9	28.8	4.5	16.7
Multimedia	40.0	41.5	10.8	0.0	7.7
Online	66.1	30.8	3.1	0.0	0.0
Video	11.5	41.0	32.7	3.3	11.5

Audio	12.9	46.8	24.2	3.2	12.9
All publications	3.3	70.5	18.0	1.6	6.6

<--- Row percents sum to 100.0% --->
(Average Base = 63)

12a. Does your company conduct market research to libraries?

Yes		44.7%
No	(SKIP TO Q.13)	55.3%
	Total:	100.0%
	Base:	76

b. How useful to you is the information provided by each of the following marketing research methods? (CIRCLE "Not applicable" IF YOU NEVER USE THE METHOD.)

	Very Useful	Moderately Useful	Somewhat Useful	Not at All Useful	Not Applicable
Focus groups	36.4%	12.1%	21.2%	0.0%	30.3%
Mail/telephone surveys	27.3	21.2	24.2	0.0	27.3
Contact at conventions	65.6	28.1	6.3	0.0	0.0
Informal visits to libraries	48.4	27.3	15.2	0.0	9.1
Librarian advisory boards	16.1	16.1	16.1	0.0	51.7
As part of sales calls	13.3	26.7	20.0	3.3	36.7
Online listserves, mail lists	21.9	15.6	21.9	3.1	37.5

<--- Row percents sum to 100.0% --->
(Average Base = 32)

13. Please rate the sales effectiveness of the following in your promotion to libraries. (RATE EACH ON A SCALE FROM 1 = "Most effective" TO 5 = "Least effective.")

	Most Effective				Least Effective
Catalogs	45.1%	42.2%	9.9%	2.8%	0.0%
Reviews	55.7	34.3	7.1	2.9	0.0
Space advertising	4.6	29.2	33.9	24.6	7.7
Title listings	9.0	22.4	44.8	17.9	6.0
Sales calls	15.0	16.7	23.3	18.3	26.7
Flyers	10.9	21.9	40.7	10.9	15.6
Direct mail	23.5	27.9	28.0	13.2	7.4
Exhibits:					
ALA	26.2	30.7	20.0	7.7	15.4
ALA–Midwinter	15.3	16.9	30.5	11.9	25.4
PLA	16.1	8.9	26.8	19.6	28.6
SLA	16.1	10.7	16.1	17.9	39.2
AASL	9.3	20.4	22.2	13.0	35.1
ACRL	9.1	7.3	18.2	18.2	47.2
State shows	7.0	26.3	28.1	19.3	19.3
Regional shows	7.3	14.5	34.6	20.0	23.6
Charleston Conference	3.9	11.8	25.5	17.6	41.2
BookExpo America	6.7	11.7	26.7	26.7	28.2
Blanket order plans	7.7	17.3	26.9	21.2	26.9
Media coverage (publicity including TV, radio, magazine, etc.)	11.1	27.1	20.6	20.6	20.6
Telemarketing	8.5	6.8	25.4	18.6	40.7
Author appearances	3.3	23.3	16.7	25.0	31.7

Library entertainment/ events	7.0	19.3	26.3	21.1	26.3
Advance readers editions	9.1	14.5	32.7	9.1	34.6
In-house publications	5.5	10.9	23.6	29.1	30.9
Online catalogs and Web sites	9.2	32.3	33.9	12.3	12.3

<--- Row percents sum to 100.0% --->
(Average Base = 60)

14a. How effective are each of the following publications as a REVIEW SOURCE (to spur library sales)?

Publication As REVIEW SOURCE

	Very Effective				Not at All Effective
Library Journal	66.7%	19.7%	4.5%	3.0%	6.1%
School LJ	57.7	21.2	5.8	3.8	11.5
Choice	48.4	29.3	10.3	3.4	8.6
Booklist/RBB	57.8	23.4	9.4	4.7	4.7
American Libraries	17.0	25.6	23.4	10.6	23.4
Publishers Weekly	49.3	13.4	14.9	13.4	9.0
Billboard	2.7	5.4	16.2	16.2	59.5
Audiofile	2.9	14.7	11.8	20.6	50.0
NYT/NYT Book Review	44.8	15.5	19.0	6.9	13.8
RQ	8.1	16.2	21.6	16.2	37.9
Information Today	6.1	6.1	21.2	18.2	48.4
Booklinks	10.3	33.3	12.8	10.3	33.3
Librarian's Yellow Pages	0.0	7.5	10.0	22.5	60.0
Horn Book	12.8	33.3	12.8	2.6	38.5
VOYA	15.8	31.6	13.2	7.9	31.5

Against the Grain	0.0	20.5	25.6	15.4	38.5
Web sites:					
Bookwire	8.8	2.9	17.6	17.7	53.0
Amazon.com	16.0	16.0	32.0	24.0	12.0
B & N Web site	11.1	15.6	26.7	28.8	17.8
Rettig on Reference	15.6	15.6	12.5	6.3	50.0
B & T publications	6.8	25.0	22.7	18.2	27.3
Ingram publications	8.7	17.4	23.9	17.4	32.6
Brodart publication	9.8	17.1	21.9	22.0	29.2
Bowker BIP outserts	0.0	5.6	11.1	25.0	58.3

<--- Row percents sum to 100.0% --->
(Average Base = 45)

14b. How effective are each of the following publications as a SPACE ADVERTISING VEHICLE?

Publication As SPACE ADVERTISING VEHICLE

	Very Effective				Not at All Effective
Library Journal	28.9%	19.2%	25.0%	11.5%	15.4%
School LJ	28.7	21.4	23.8	7.1	19.0
Choice	18.8	20.8	25.0	14.6	20.8
Booklist/RBB	25.5	29.8	21.3	12.8	10.6
American Libraries	7.3	12.2	17.1	34.1	29.3
Publishers Weekly	17.3	17.3	23.1	19.2	23.1
Billboard	0.0	3.4	13.8	17.2	65.6
Audiofile	3.7	11.1	7.4	14.8	63.0
NYT/NYT Book Review	19.0	16.7	19.0	19.0	26.3

RQ	0.0	6.3	18.8	31.2	43.7
Information Today	3.2	9.7	16.1	22.6	48.4
Booklinks	6.1	21.2	21.2	15.2	36.3
Librarian's Yellow Pages	0.0	5.4	13.5	21.6	59.5
Horn Book	3.1	21.9	25.0	9.4	40.6
VOYA	3.0	12.1	24.2	18.2	42.5
Against the Grain	2.7	5.4	24.3	24.3	43.3
Web sites:					
Bookwire	0.0	6.5	16.1	16.1	61.3
Amazon.com	5.3	18.4	18.4	23.7	34.2
B & N Web site	5.6	16.7	19.4	19.4	38.9
Rettig on Reference	3.6	10.7	10.7	7.1	67.9
B & T publications	7.5	20.0	32.5	15.0	25.0
Ingram publications	12.2	19.5	17.1	22.0	29.2
Brodart publication	8.1	13.5	29.7	16.2	32.5
Bowker BIP outserts	0.0	10.8	18.9	16.2	54.1

<--- Row percents sum to 100.0% --->
(Average Base = 38)

15. Are your sales to libraries ever hurt by:

	Yes	No	Total	Base
Unfavorable reviews?	67.6%	32.4	100.0%	68
Noncommittal reviews?	35.4%	64.6	100.0%	65

16. Do you participate in:

	Yes	No	Total	Base
Cataloging in publication CIP?	83.6%	16.4	100.0%	73

International Standard Book Number (ISBN)?	98.7%	1.3	100.0%	77	
UPC?	54.5%	45.5	100.0%	66	
EAN Booklan coding?	66.7%	33.3	100.0%	69	

17. What kind of timing has proven most effective in your promotion to libraries of the following materials? (CIRCLE "Does not apply" IF PROMOTION IS NOT USED.)

	6 Months before	3 Months before	1 Month before	At Publi-cation	Post-Publi-cation	Does Not Apply
Bound galleys	7.1%	21.4%	4.3%	1.4%	0.0%	65.8%
Posters/point of sale	3.0	3.0	1.5	11.9	9.0	71.6
Seasonal catalogs	19.7	42.3	11.3	7.0	5.6	14.1
Subject brochures	2.9	24.3	5.7	22.9	15.7	28.5
Single title flyers	4.3	18.8	8.7	18.8	8.7	40.7
Newsletters	9.0	6.0	7.5	8.9	4.5	64.1
E-mail/Web site	8.5	12.7	9.9	25.3	9.9	33.7
Trade advertising	4.8	19.4	12.9	16.1	14.5	32.3

< - - - Row percents sum to 100.0% - - - >
(Average Base = 68)

18. Does your company use a sales force for the library market?

Yes		26.3%
No	(SKIP TO Q.20)	73.7%
	Total:	100.0%
	Base:	76

19a. What type(s) of sales force do you use? (CIRCLE ALL THAT APPLY.)

House field representatives	33.3%
House telemarketing representatives	42.9%
National representatives	14.3%
Management	14.3%
Exclusive commission group	9.5%
Nonexclusive commission group	61.9%
Outside telesales group	9.5%
Other	0.0%
Base:	77

b. What tasks do you expect your sales reps to accomplish on a library sales call? (RATE EACH TASK ON A SCALE FROM 1= "Highest priority" TO 5 = "Lowest priority.")

	Highest Priority				Lowest Priority
Present new titles	80.0%	10.0%	5.0%	0.0%	5.0%
Take orders	50.0	15.0	10.0	5.0	20.0
Troubleshoot problems	5.0	35.0	20.0	20.0	20.0
Provide special services	10.5	15.8	31.6	10.5	31.6
Discuss special services	20.0	15.0	25.0	20.0	20.0
Discuss market research	5.0	10.0	30.0	30.0	25.0
Discuss publishing trends	5.3	15.8	36.8	15.8	26.3

<--- Row percents sum to 100.0% --->
(Average Base = 20)

(QUESTION 20 WAS OMITTED WHEN SURVEY WAS PRINTED BY CLIENT)

20. Do you currently sell to consortia or library purchasing groups?

        Yes
        No   (SKIP TO Q.25)

21a. Do you have sales/marketing staff devoted to working with consortia or library purchasing groups?

Yes		9.2%
No	(SKIP TO Q.22)	90.8%
	Total:	100.0%
	Base:	76

(IF "YES"):

b. What are the title(s) of these sales/marketing staff:
Responses not provided.

22. What percentage of your sales is generated by consortia or library purchasing groups?

0 percent		31.6%
1 percent		7.0%
2 percent		5.3%
3 percent		1.8%
5 percent		5.3%
6 percent		1.8%
10 percent		14.0%
100 percent		1.6%
Don't Know		31.6%
	Total:	100.0%
	Base:	57

23. If you offer discounts to consortia, please indicate the *most* common method of discounting:

Lower per–FTE price		3.1%
Volume discounts with sliding scale discount		25.0%
Flat-rate discount		18.8%
Do not offer discounts to consortia		43.7%
Other		9.4%
	Total:	100.0%
	Base:	32

24. What impact have consortial or library purchasing groups had on your overall sales $ volume?

Positive impact	18.9%
Negative impact	1.9%
Not sure	79.2%
Total:	100.0%
Base:	53

25. How important will consortia and library purchasing groups be to your business in the next three to five years?

Very important	19.2%
Moderately important	13.5%
Somewhat important	46.1%
Not at all important	21.2%
Total:	100.0%
Base:	52

26. Which of the following people represent your company at library exhibits? (CIRCLE ALL THAT APPLY.)

Senior management	58.4%
Sales personnel	39.0%
Editors	36.4%
Marketing personnel	59.7%
Customer service groups	7.8%
Other	9.1%
Base:	77

27. Do you publish the same title in multiple formats?

	Usually	Sometimes	Never
Hardcover/paperback simultaneously	18.6%	50.0%	31.4%
Hardcover/paperback a year apart	11.9	50.8	37.3
Book/audio	1.6	37.1	61.3
Book/electronic or CD–ROM	3.2	30.6	66.2
Book/online	3.3	15.0	81.7
Book/video	1.7	11.9	86.4

Book/large type	0.0	10.7	89.3
Foreign language/English	3.3	35.0	61.7

<--- Row percents sum to 100.0% --->
(Average Base = 62)

28a. During the past two years, what changes have you noticed in multiple copy purchases by libraries of the following:

	Increased	Decreased	No Change
Trade hardcover	31.6%	21.1%	47.3%
Trade paperback	46.4	7.3	46.3
Juvenile cloth	36.7	13.3	50.0
Juvenile paper	41.4	6.9	51.7
Reference	25.6	27.9	46.5
Electronic reference	28.0	8.0	64.0
Professional/technical	10.7	25.0	64.3
University press	4.3	26.1	69.6
CD-ROM	25.9	14.8	59.3
Audio	39.1	4.3	56.6
Video	5.3	5.3	89.4

<--- Row percents sum to 100.0% --->
(Average Base = 30)

b. Rate the factors that you think drive multiple copy purchases by libraries (per each location):

	Always a Factor				Never a Factor
Best-seller titles	72.4%	15.5%	5.2%	0.0%	6.9%
Oprah/celebrity endorses	59.6	24.6	5.3	0.0	10.5
Book awards/ prizes	35.6	40.7	20.3	1.7	1.7
Announced promos/tours	3.5	19.3	43.9	15.8	17.5
Price of book	14.5	30.6	27.4	21.0	6.5
Library funding	56.9	32.3	10.8	0.0	0.0
Publisher in-print policy	1.8	30.4	37.5	21.4	8.9

Interlibrary loan	7.3	25.5	41.8	14.5	10.9

<--- Row percents sum to 100.0% --->
(Average Base = 59)

29. What services do you supply for librarians? (CIRCLE ALL THAT APPLY.)

EDI invoicing	4.3%
EDI payment	10.4%
Fax ordering	96.1%
Online ordering	49.4%
Customer relations representatives	68.8%
Preprocessing	18.2%
Other	6.5%
Base:	77

30. Do you prefer that libraries order direct or through a vendor?

Prefer direct	45.4%
Prefer through vendor	13.0%
No preference	40.3%
Don't allow direct	1.3%
Don't allow vendor	0.0%
Total:	100.0%
Base:	77

31. Are returns of your materials by libraries . . .

Increasing,	4.2%
Decreasing, or	9.7%
Remaining static?	86.1%
Total:	100.0%
Base:	72

32. What are the most common reasons for library returns?

	Most Frequent				Least Frequent
Defective product	32.1%	13.6%	15.3%	13.6%	25.4%

Shipping damage	25.9	25.8	17.2	19.0	12.1
Duplicate shipment by publisher/vendor	7.0	17.5	14.0	24.6	36.7
Picking errors	7.1	7.1	21.4	28.6	35.6
Price increase	0.0	1.9	7.5	22.6	68.0
Wrong item sent	13.3	16.7	23.3	25.0	21.7
Wrong shipping address	3.7	0.0	16.7	29.6	50.0
Approval plan	5.8	3.8	21.2	19.2	50.0
Wrong title ordered	1.8	1.8	32.1	33.9	30.4
Inappropriate material	0.0	3.7	3.7	25.9	66.7
Duplicate order by library	3.4	5.2	25.9	29.3	36.2
Incorrect processing	1.9	3.8	19.2	21.2	53.7

<--- Row percents sum to 100.0% --->
(Average Base = 56)

33. Are returns of your materials by vendors ...

Increasing,	17.9%
Decreasing, or	19.4%
Remaining static?	62.7%
Total:	100.0%
Base:	67

34. What are the most common reasons for vendor returns?

	Most Frequent				Least Frequent
Defective product	17.0%	15.1%	11.3%	28.3%	28.3%
Shipping damage	16.4	21.8	18.2	36.3	7.3
Duplicate shipment					

by publisher/vendor	1.9	15.1	15.1	26.4	41.5
Picking errors	8.0	6.0	24.0	30.0	32.0
Price increase	0.0	0.0	12.2	28.6	59.2
Wrong item sent	9.4	9.4	20.8	24.5	35.9
Wrong shipping address	0.0	6.0	8.0	18.0	68.0
Approval plan	8.5	4.3	17.0	10.6	59.6
Wrong title ordered	3.8	13.5	19.2	30.8	32.7
Inappropriate material	0.0	4.3	10.6	14.9	70.2
Duplicate order by library	3.9	5.9	21.6	13.7	54.9
Incorrect processing	2.1	4.3	10.6	14.9	68.1

<--- Row percents sum to 100.0% --->
(Average Base = 51)

35. What percentage of your new titles (by category) are published on the announced date?

	0–15%	16–35%	36–80%	Over 80%
Trade hardcover	4.5%	9.1%	38.6%	47.8%
Trade paperback	4.8	7.1	35.7	52.4
Juvenile cloth	4.2	12.5	16.7	66.6
Juvenile paper	4.0	8.0	24.0	64.0
Reference	7.3	17.1	36.6	39.0
Electronic reference	13.3	20.0	6.7	60.0
Professional/technical	8.3	8.3	29.2	54.2
University press	0.0	7.1	42.9	50.0
CD–ROM	21.1	26.3	15.8	36.8
Audio	7.1	21.4	21.4	50.1
Video	11.1	33.3	11.1	44.5

<--- Row percents sum to 100.0% --->
(Average Base = 25)

36. On average, how long (in months) do your materials in these categories stay in print?

	Over 1–6 Mo	7–12 Mo	13–18 Mo	19–24 Mo	24–Mo
Trade hardcover	0.0%	0.0%	2.1%	10.6%	87.3%
Trade paperback	0.0	0.0	4.3	6.4	89.3
Juvenile cloth	0.0	0.0	3.8	3.8	92.4
Juvenile paper	0.0	0.0	3.7	0.0	96.3
Reference	0.0	0.0	2.3	2.3	95.4
Electronic reference	0.0	12.5	12.5	0.0	75.0
Professional/ technical	0.0	0.0	8.0	4.0	88.0
University press	0.0	0.0	0.0	14.3	85.7
CD–ROM	0.0	18.2	9.1	0.0	72.7
Audio	0.0	7.1	0.0	14.3	78.6
Video	0.0	10.0	10.0	20.0	60.0

<---- Row percents sum to 100.0% ---->
(Average Base = 26)

37. How do you rate the usefulness of the following information in processing orders from libraries? (RATE EACH ON A SCALE FROM 1 = "Most useful" TO 5 = "Least useful.")

	Most Useful				Least Useful	Don't Use
ISBN	90.2%	2.8%	2.8%	1.4%	2.8%	0.0%
ISSN	20.2	10.2	13.6	6.8	3.4	45.8
SAN	11.1	3.7	7.4	7.4	9.3	61.1
LCCN	7.5	3.8	13.2	1.9	5.7	67.9
SKU	7.7	5.8	9.6	1.9	7.7	67.3
Title	69.0	26.8	1.4	1.4	0.0	1.4
Edition	39.9	21.4	14.3	2.9	8.6	12.9
Binding	31.4	20.9	14.9	6.0	11.9	14.9
Price	18.8	17.4	26.2	15.9	13.0	8.7

Customer
account
number   44.6   27.7   12.3   3.1   3.1   9.2

< - - - Row percents sum to 100.0% - - - >
(Average Base = 63)

38. Please feel free to comment further on any questions or problems that were dealt with in this questionnaire.

— I would need input from 2–3 other people in other offices to adequately answer all your questions. We don't have staff dedicated to library sales.

— This questionnaire is extremely BOOKS oriented. With journals representing the lion's share of research libraries' materials budgets, journals should be a more significant factor in the survey. Also, issues involving print—electronic are more pressing to libraries (or ALCTS members) than author book tours!

— We don't normally market to libraries. I have very little information about who to market to, or how successful/viable of a market this is for textbooks. I'd like additional information. Thank you.

— I'm sorry I could not answer many of the questions—we simply don't hold this information! But something to think about for the future.

— As a publisher of STM books and journals (90 books in '98, 16 journals) we make a large percentage of sales to libraries, but most are through library jobbers such as YBP or BNA. Much of our demand is generated by a combination of faculty recommendations, approval plans, and state-of-the art publications at the forefront of medical science.

10

AAP/ALCTS Library Marketing Survey: Vendor Questionnaire

1. Which categories best describe your products/services? (CIRCLE ALL THAT APPLY.)

Audio	33.3%
Visual	25.0%
Book and paper mending/ preservation services	0.0%
Book distribution	10.0%
Book publisher	8.3%
Cataloging services	41.7%
CD-ROM publisher	0.0%
Computer hardware	0.0%
Computer software	8.3%
Consulting services	0.0%
Data conversion services	0.0%
Data entry/preparation	0.0%
Database information products	16.7%
Document delivery services	0.0%
Electronic journals	0.0%
Facilities management	0.0%
Financial services	0.0%
Furniture/shelving	0.0%
Internet/Intranet/Web site services	8.3%
Leasing	8.3%
Library information systems	0.0%

Multimedia	8.3%
Online services	33.3%
Supplies	0.0%
Training	0.0%
Other	0.0%
Base:	12

2a. Is there a division (or divisions) within your company devoted exclusively to library sales?

Yes	81.8%
No	18.2% (SKIP TO Q.3)
Total:	100.0%
Base:	11

b. About how many employees are devoted exclusively to library sales?

1	10.0%
4	10.0%
7	20.0%
10	10.0%
12	10.0%
30	10.0%
240	10.0%
380	10.0%
625	10.0%
Total:	100.0%
Base:	10

c. About what percentage of your employees are devoted exclusively to library sales?

3	20.0%
5	10.0%
6	10.0%
10	10.0%
15	10.0%
50	10.0%
100	30.0%

Total:	100.0%
Base:	10

3a. Does your company have a library marketing budget?

Yes	100.0%	
No	0.0%	(SKIP TO Q.5)
Total:	100.0%	
Base:	10	

b. Is your library marketing budget based on a percentage of total sales?

Yes	30.0%
No	70.0%
Total:	100.0%
Base:	10

4. What percentage of your library marketing budget is spent in each of the following categories? (IF UNSURE, GIVE YOUR BEST ESTIMATE.)

	Average Percent
Direct mail	2.0%
Telemarketing	1.7%
Sales representatives	54.7%
Catalogs	4.5%
Publicity	2.2%
Space advertising	5.8%
Exhibits:	
State	4.1%
Regional	4.1%
National	13.0%
Flyers	1.3%
Newsletters	3.3%
Web site	2.9%
Other	0.4%
Total:	100.0%
Base:	10

Other = Media

5. Which of the following best describes the amount of your annual dollar sales to libraries?

Under $1 million		8.3%
$1 million to $5 million		33.3%
$5 million to $15 million		0.0%
$15 million to $30 million		16.7%
$30 million to $50 million		8.3%
Over $50 million		33.3%
	Total:	100.0%
	Base:	12

6. About what percentage of your total annual sales is to libraries?

5 percent		8.3%
10 percent		8.3%
35 percent		8.3%
60 percent		8.3%
80 percent		8.3%
95 percent		16.7%
97 percent		8.3%
100 percent		33.3%
	Total:	100.0%
	Base:	10

7. About what percentage of your total library sales is to each of the following types of libraries? (IF UNSURE, GIVE YOUR BEST ESTIMATE.)

	Average Percent
ARL library	11.3%
College/university (other than ARL)	19.6%
Two-year college	4.8%
Public	20.2%
Special (SPECIFY, e.g., medicine, law, art, corporate, etc.)	28.2%
School (SPECIFY, e.g., K–8, 9–12, academic, vocational-technical)	12.9%
Government	3.0%

Total:	100.0%
Base:	12

Other (special) = Medicine (two responses)
　　　　　　　　Corporate (two responses)
Other (school) = K–12
　　　　　　　　K–8, 9–12

8. About what percentage of your total library sales is in each of the following geographic regions? (IF UNSURE, GIVE YOUR BEST ESTIMATE.)

	Average Percent
United States:	
Northeast	28.6%
Southeast	18.0%
North central	14.0%
South central	10.7%
Northwest	7.3%
Southwest	13.7%
Canada	1.6%
Latin America	0.2%
Pacific Rim	1.5%
Australia/New Zealand	0.9%
Europe	1.6%
Middle East	1.1%
Africa	0.6%
Other (SPECIFY)	0.2%
Total:	100.0%
Base:	12

Other = Caribbean and misc.

9. What percentages of your library sales consist of . . .
　　U.S. published materials?

2 percent	8.3%
70 percent	8.3%
80 percent	16.7%
90 percent	16.7%

95 percent		25.0%
99 percent		16.7%
100 percent		8.3%
	Total:	100.0%
	Base:	12

Non–U.S. published materials?

1 percent		18.2%
5 percent		27.3%
10 percent		18.2%
20 percent		18.2%
30 percent		9.1%
98 percent		9.1%
	Total:	100.0%
	Base:	11

10. What percentage of your library sales in each category is made to the following types of library? See table on p. 113.
(Average percent)

11. About what percentage of your total library sales fall into each of the following categories? (IF UNSURE, GIVE YOUR BEST ESTIMATE.)

	Average Percent
Monographs (trade/popular)	31.9%
Monographs (scholarly/technical)	46.9
Multivolume reference	6.6
Periodicals/serials	2.7
Nonbook (e.g., filmstrips)	0.3
Large print books	0.4
Computer software (program)	0.4
Computer software (content)	1.3
Electronic database	0.5
Microforms	0.0
Video formats	2.9
Sound recordings	0.6
Other	5.5

	None	ARL Lib.	Coll./Univ.	Two-yr. Coll.	Pub.	Spec.	School K-12	Gov.	Total
Monographs (trade/popular)	9.1%	17.2	21.7	2.2	8.8	28.6	10.7	1.7	100.0%
Monographs scholarly/technical)	9.1%	13.2	19.1	3.3	12.1	24.3	3.9	5.0	100.0%
Multivolume reference	18.2%	15.0	19.1	3.3	10.0	19.8	13.9	.7	100.0%
Periodicals/serials	63.6%	10.9	5.8	.5	0.0	9.6	9.1	.5	100.0%
Nonbook (e.g., filmstrips)	91.7%	0.0	0.0	0.0	0.0	0.0	8.3	0.0	100.0%
Large print books	75.0%	0.0	0.0	0.0	16.7	0.0	8.3	0.0	100.0%
Computer software (program)	100.0%	0.0	0.0	0.0	0.0	0.0	0.0	0.0	100.0%
Computer software (content)	63.7%	0.0	0.9	0.5	4.0	18.0	12.7	0.2	100.0%
Electronic database	90.9%	0.0	0.0	0.0	0.0	8.9	0.0	0.2	100.0%
Microforms	100.0%	0.0	0.0	0.0	0.0	0.0	0.0	0.0	100.0%
Video formats	45.5%	5.4	22.3	5.4	1.4	10.0	9.4	0.6	100.0%
Sound recordings	72.7%	1.8	8.6	0.9	4.6	10.0	0.3	1.1	100.0%
Other	91.7%	6.0	0.9	0.0	0.0	0.0	0.0	1.4	100.0%

Other = Books

	Total:	100.0%
	Base:	12

12. About what percentage of your total library sales do the following categories represent?

	Average Percent
Firm orders	77.8%
Blanket orders or automatic shipment	4.8%
Approval plan orders	8.8%
Standing orders	6.8%
Subscriptions	0.1%
Leasing	1.7%
Other	0.0%
Total:	100.0%
Base:	12

13. Please rate the effectiveness of each of the following factors on your sales to libraries. (RATE EACH ON A SCALE FROM 1 = "Most effective" TO 5 = "Least effective.")

	Most Effective				Least Effective
Price	25.0%	25.0%	33.3%	8.3%	8.3%
Binding quality	9.1	9.1	45.5	9.1	27.3
Type of binding	9.1	18.2	36.4	9.1	27.3
Discount	33.3	33.3	16.7	8.3	8.3
Reviews	10.0	40.0	40.0	0.0	10.0
Toll-free 800 numbers	16.7	50.0	16.7	8.3	8.3
Online capabilities (E-mail, Web site, database)	50.0	33.3	8.3	0.0	8.3
Co-op advertising	8.3	16.7	16.7	16.7	41.7
Prepub/special pricing	16.7	25.0	16.7	16.7	25.0
Use of premiums	0.0	16.7	16.7	33.3	33.3
Stock availability	16.7	41.7	16.7	16.7	8.3

	1	2	3	4	5
Bibliographic data (e.g., CIP, BIP, MARC)	36.4	36.4	18.2	0.0	9.1
Shelf-ready processing services	36.4	18.2	27.3	0.0	18.2
Library networks (e.g., OCLC, WLN, RLG)	0.0	27.3	27.3	18.2	27.3
Quality of service:					
Timeliness	75.0	16.7	0.0	8.3	0.0
Accuracy	66.7	25.0	0.0	8.3	0.0
Fill rate	54.5	36.4	0.0	9.1	0.0
Sales representatives	45.5	27.3	9.1	9.1	9.1
Vendor database	25.0	33.3	0.0	33.3	8.3
Collection development services	41.7	8.3	8.3	25.0	16.7
Customer service representatives	58.3	33.3	8.3	0.0	0.0

<‑ ‑ ‑ Row percents sum to 100.0% ‑ ‑ ‑>
(Average Base = 12)

13a. Please specify other factors that affect your sales to libraries.
    Other = Referrals

14a. Please rate the sales effectiveness of the following in your promotion to libraries. (RATE EACH ON A SCALE FROM 1 = "Most effective" TO 5 = "Least effective.")

	Most Effective				Least Effective
Catalogs	27.3%	9.1%	27.3%	9.1%	27.3%
Reviews	20.0	10.0	30.0	0.0	40.0
Space advertising	0.0	9.1	36.4	9.1	45.5

Title listings	10.0	30.0	20.0	20.0	20.0
Sales calls	72.7	8.3	8.3	0.0	8.3
Flyers	9.1	36.4	54.5	0.0	0.0
Direct mail	8.3	41.7	33.3	16.7	0.0
Exhibits:					
ALA	0.0	18.2	54.5	0.0	27.3
ALA–Midwinter	0.0	10.0	50.0	0.0	40.0
PLA	10.0	0.0	10.0	10.0	70.0
SLA	9.1	9.1	18.2	18.2	45.5
AASL	11.1	11.1	11.1	11.1	55.6
ACRL	0.0	10.0	20.0	10.0	60.0
State shows	0.0	30.0	20.0	30.0	20.0
Regional shows	0.0	36.4	18.2	27.3	18.2
Charleston Conference	10.0	10.0	20.0	20.0	40.0
BookExpo America	0.0	0.0	9.1	18.2	72.7
Blanket order plans	20.0	30.0	10.0	0.0	40.0
Media coverage (publicity including TV, radio, magazine, etc.)	0.0	0.0	0.0	20.0	80.0
Telemarketing	10.0	30.0	0.0	10.0	50.0
Author appearances	0.0	0.0	0.0	20.0	80.0
Library entertainment/ events	0.0	0.0	20.0	20.0	60.0
Advance readers editions	0.0	0.0	0.0	11.1	88.9
In-house publications	0.0	20.0	10.0	20.0	50.0
Online catalogs and Web sites	36.4	27.3	27.3	9.1	0.0

<--- Row percents sum to 100.0% --->
(Average Base = 10)

14a. Please specify other promotional methods.
Other = Word of mouth

b. From Q.14a above, choose the five most important methods and list them below in order of importance (1 = *most important*).

METHOD	#1 Most Important Method	#2 Most Important Method	#3 Most Important Method	#4 Most Important Method	#5 Most Important Method
Catalogs	—	8.3%	8.3%	8.3%	—
Reviews	—	—	16.7	—	9.1
Space advertising	—	—	8.3	—	—
Title listings	—	8.3	—	8.3	—
Sales calls	66.7	—	—	8.3	—
Flyers	—	—	—	8.3	27.3
Direct mail	—	8.3	—	16.7	9.1
Exhibits: ALA	—	—	—	8.3	—
Exhibits: ALA–Midwinter	—	—	—	8.3	9.1
Exhibits: PLA	—	—	—	—	9.1
Exhibits: SLA	—	8.3	—	8.3	—
Exhibits: AASL	—	—	—	—	—
Exhibits: ACRL	—	—	8.3	—	—
Exhibits: State shows	—	—	—	—	9.1
Exhibits: Regional shows	8.3	—	—	—	—
Exhibits: Charleston Con.	—	—	8.3	—	—
Exhibits: BookExpo America	—	—	—	—	—
Blanket order plans	—	8.3	16.7	—	18.2
Media coverage	—	—	—	—	—
Telemarketing	8.3	16.7	—	—	—
Author appearances	—	—	—	—	—

Other responses	Referrals	Word of mouth	News-letter	MLA attendance	Collection develop. services
Library entertainment/ events	—	—	—	—	—
Advance readers editions	8.3	—	—	—	—
In-house publications	—	—	—	—	9.1
Online catalogs/ Web sites	—	25.0	25.0	16.7	—
TOTAL OF OTHER METHODS	8.3	16.7	8.3	8.3	—
BASE	12	12	12	12	11
BLANKS	0	0	0	0	1

15. To which of the following do you apply shipping charges? (CIRCLE ALL THAT APPLY.)

Electronic orders	50.0%
Single-copy orders	50.0%
Approval plan orders	8.3%
Mail orders	50.0%
Rush orders	75.0%
Secondary warehouse orders	25.0%
Standing orders and subscriptions	33.3%
Export shipping	58.3%
NONE OF THE ABOVE	8.3%
Base:	12

16. Excluding value-added programs (e.g., cataloging and processing), what is your policy on book returns from libraries? (CIRCLE ONE)

Processed without charge	33.3%
Processed without charge if resalable or returnable to publisher	58.3%

Processed with a service charge		8.3%
Returns not permitted		0.0%
	Total:	100.0%
	Base:	12

17. Please estimate the approximate returns (percent) for the following types of sales:

	1–5%	6–10%	11–15%	> 15%	Total	Base
Firm orders	100.0	0.0	0.0	0.0	100.0%	12
Blanket orders or automatic adjustment	42.9	57.1	0.0	0.0	100.0%	7
Approval plan orders	42.9	42.9	0.0	14.3	100.0%	7
Standing orders	100.0	0.0	0.0	0.0	100.0%	9
Continuations	100.0	0.0	0.0	0.0	100.0%	7
Subscriptions	0.0	0.0	0.0	0.0	0.0	0
Leasing	0.0	0.0	0.0	100.0	100.0%	1

18. For each of the following types of sales, are library returns increasing, decreasing, or remaining static?

	Increasing	Decreasing	Remaining Static	Total	Base
Firm orders	0.0	8.3	91.7	100.0%	12
Blanket orders or automatic shipment	12.5	25.0	62.5	100.0%	8
Approval plan orders	14.3	14.3	71.4	100.0%	7
Standing orders	0.0	0.0	100.0	100.0%	10
Continuations	0.0	0.0	100.0	100.0%	8
Subscriptions	0.0	0.0	100.0	100.0%	1
Leasing	0.0	0.0	100.0	100.0%	2
Other	0.0	0.0	100.0	100.0%	1

19. What are the most common reasons for library returns?

	Most Frequent				Least Frequent
Defective product	55.6%	0.0%	11.1%	22.2%	11.1%
Shipping damage	22.2	44.4	0.0	33.3	0.0
Duplicate shipment by vendor	36.4	9.1	9.1	18.2	27.3
Picking errors	22.2	0.0	44.4	11.1	22.2
Price increase	0.0	0.0	0.0	11.1	88.9
Wrong item sent	36.4	0.0	45.5	9.1	9.1
Wrong shipping address	0.0	0.0	12.5	12.5	75.0
Approval plan	83.3	0.0	0.0	16.7	0.0
Wrong title ordered	36.4	27.3	9.1	27.3	0.0
Inappropriate material	28.6	0.0	0.0	42.9	28.6
Duplicate order by library	33.3	11.1	11.1	44.4	0.0
Incorrect processing	0.0	0.0	12.5	87.5	0.0

<--- Row percents sum to 100.0% --->
(Average Base = 9)

19a. Please specify other reason for library returns.
Other = Surplus

20. Please rate the sales effectiveness of the following types of value-added services. (RATE EACH ON A SCALE FROM 1 = "Most effective" TO 5 = "Least effective.")

	Most Effective				Least Effective
Preprocessing	50.0%	10.0%	10.0%	20.0%	10.0%
Paperback prebinding	30.0	0.0	30.0	10.0	30.0
Processing kits	20.0	20.0	20.0	0.0	40.0
Catalog cards	30.0	0.0	30.0	10.0	30.0
Machine-readable record delivery	50.0	0.0	10.0	0.0	40.0
Record enrichment	30.0	20.0	20.0	0.0	30.0
Blanket orders	22.2	22.2	0.0	22.2	33.3
Approval plan orders	50.0	12.5	0.0	12.5	25.0
Standing orders	36.4	36.4	9.1	9.1	9.1
Subscriptions	0.0	0.0	0.0	16.7	83.3
Other continuations	22.2	22.2	11.1	0.0	44.4
Fund accounting	30.0	0.0	30.0	10.0	30.0
Order prepayment options	30.0	20.0	20.0	20.0	10.0
Confirming order slips	10.0	20.0	40.0	20.0	10.0
Online order service	54.5	27.3	9.1	9.1	0.0

<--- Row percents sum to 100.0% --->
(Average Base = 10)

20a. Please specify other value-added service.
    Other = Newsletter

21. What percentage of your library sales in each value-added service category is made to the following types of library? (Average percent) See table on p. 123.

21a. Please specify other value-added service categories.
Other = Newsletter

22. Which ordering tools do you provide to each type of library? (CIRCLE ALL THAT APPLY IN EACH COLUMN; CIRCLE 0 = "Do not provide" IF APPROPRIATE.) See table on p. 124

23. How important do you think different factors are to librarians in deciding to buy from a vendor? (RATE EACH ON A SCALE FROM 1 = "Very important" TO 5 = "Not at all important.")

	Very Important				Not at All Important
Price	45.5%	36.4%	0.0%	0.0%	18.2%
Discount	54.5	36.4	0.0	9.1	0.0
Reviews	11.1	11.1	33.3	33.3	11.1
Reputation of author	0.0	50.0	0.0	12.5	37.5
Reputation of vendor	66.7	25.0	0.0	0.0	8.3
Inclusion on recommended lists and awards	0.0	42.9	14.3	14.3	28.6
Media coverage	0.0	14.3	14.3	28.6	42.9
Web site, online publicity, and information	27.3	54.5	18.2	0.0	0.0
Author tours	0.0	0.0	0.0	28.6	71.4
Binding quality	22.2	0.0	33.3	22.2	22.2
Binding type	22.2	11.1	22.2	22.2	22.2
Acid free paper	12.5	25.0	12.5	12.5	37.5
Bibliographic tools like CIP, BIP	30.0	20.0	30.0	0.0	20.0
Overall reputation of publisher or imprint	25.0	25.0	12.5	0.0	37.5
Free freight	54.5	18.2	18.2	9.1	0.0
Customer service	81.8	9.1	9.1	0.0	0.0

	None	ARL Lib.	Coll./ Univ.	Two-yr. Coll.	Pub.	Spec.	School K-12	Gov.	Total
Preprocessing	33.3%	8.6	21.3	0.8	7.0	9.4	19.4	0.2	100.0%
Paperback prebinding	41.7%	8.3	25.0	5.0	7.5	1.2	11.1	0.2	100.0%
Processing kits	58.3%	2.9	10.0	0.8	2.9	.8	23.6	0.7	100.0%
Catalog cards	41.7%	2.5	10.4	0.8	2.5	17.1	23.6	1.4	100.0%
Machine-readable record delivery	50.0%	10.4	19.2	0.8	3.9	1.1	14.4	0.2	100.0%
Record enrichment	58.3%	9.6	14.6	0.0	8.9	0.3	8.3	0.0	100.0%
Blanket orders	50.0%	8.3	11.7	4.2	9.2	16.2	0.0	0.4	100.0%
Approval plan orders	58.3%	12.5	11.7	0.0	.6	16.7	0.0	0.2	100.0%
Standing orders	25.0%	14.6	17.5	5.4	11.0	26.1	0.2	0.2	100.0%
Subscriptions	100.0%	0.0	0.0	0.0	0.0	0.0	0.0	0.0	100.0%
Other continuations	66.7%	3.3	7.9	4.6	9.2	8.3	0.0	0.0	100.0%
Fund accounting	58.3%	9.2	6.7	0.0	1.6	17.5	6.7	0.0	100.0%
Order prepayment options	33.3%	13.8	12.1	3.3	10.8	26.7	0.0	0.0	100.0%
Confirming order slips	58.3%	7.9	7.1	0.0	7.5	8.8	10.0	0.4	100.0%
Online order service	33.3%	12.1	19.2	5.0	9.2	17.9	1.9	1.4	100.0%
Other	91.7%	0.0	0.0	0.0	0.0	8.3	0.0	0.0	100.0%

	Do Not Provide	ARL Lib.	Coll./ Univ.	Two-yr. Coll.	Pub.	Spec.	School K–12	Gov.
Microfiche	50.0%	8.3%	16.7%	16.7%	16.7%	16.7%	8.3%	8.3%
Hardcopy listings	33.3%	16.7%	33.3%	33.3%	25.0%	41.7%	25.0%	16.7%
Magazines, catalogs, etc.	16.7%	8.3%	33.3%	25.0%	25.0%	16.7%	25.0%	16.7%
Online/Internet access	8.3%	50.0%	58.3%	58.3%	58.3%	66.7%	50.0%	50.0%
Announcement slips	16.7%	33.3%	33.3%	33.3%	25.0%	41.7%	0.0%	25.0%
CD-ROM	41.7%	8.3%	16.7%	16.7%	16.7%	16.7%	25.0%	8.3%
E-mail notice of new titles	25.0%	25.0%	33.3%	25.0%	16.7%	16.7%	8.3%	0.0%

<--- Base for all of above = 12 --->

On-time shipping with adequate packing standards	72.7	9.1	18.2	0.0	0.0
EDI capability	22.2	33.3	11.1	33.3	0.0
Toll-free 800 numbers	72.7	9.1	18.2	0.0	0.0
Telemarketing	18.2	9.1	9.1	27.3	36.4
Sales representatives	66.7	0.0	25.0	0.0	8.3
Availability of standing orders	45.5	18.2	18.2	0.0	18.2
Preprocessing services	45.5	18.2	18.2	9.1	9.1
Promotional materials	9.1	27.3	54.5	9.1	0.0
Direct mail	8.3	8.3	33.3	41.7	8.3

<--- Row percents sum to 100.0% --->
(Average Base = 10)

24. What do you expect your representatives to accomplish on library sales calls? (CIRCLE ALL THAT APPLY.)

Present new titles	33.3%
Present backlist titles	16.7%
Assist in placing orders	50.0%
Troubleshoot problems	91.7%
Provide special services	41.7%
Discuss special services	66.7%
Discuss market research	25.0%
Discuss publishing trends	41.7%
Introduce new services	66.7%
Train on electronic products	33.3%
Other	8.3%
Base:	12

24a. Please specify other tasks you expect representative to accomplish.
  Other = Relationship building/maintain existing accounts

25a. How effective are each of the following publications both as a review source (to spur library sales) and as a space advertising vehicle?

Publication As REVIEW SOURCE

	Very Effective				Not at All Effective
Library Journal	25.0%	50.0%	12.5%	0.0%	12.5%
School LJ	14.3	42.9	0.0	0.0	42.9
Choice	14.3	42.9	0.0	0.0	42.9
Booklist/RBB	28.6	14.3	14.3	14.3	28.6
American Libraries	0.0	14.3	28.6	14.3	42.9
Publishers Weekly	12.5	50.0	12.5	0.0	25.0
Billboard	0.0	0.0	28.6	14.3	57.1
Audiofile	0.0	0.0	14.3	28.6	57.1
NYT/NYT Book Review	14.3	14.3	28.6	0.0	42.9
RQ	0.0	14.3	14.3	0.0	71.4
Information Today	0.0	28.6	14.3	0.0	57.1
Booklinks	0.0	14.3	42.9	0.0	42.9
Librarian's Yellow Pages	0.0	14.3	28.6	0.0	57.1
Horn Book	0.0	42.9	14.3	0.0	42.9
VOYA	0.0	14.3	28.6	0.0	57.1
Against the Grain	0.0	0.0	14.3	28.6	57.1
Web sites:					
Bookwire	0.0	14.3	0.0	0.0	85.7
Amazon.com	12.5	0.0	37.5	12.5	37.5
B & N Web site	0.0	0.0	42.9	14.3	42.9
Rettig on Reference	28.6	0.0	14.3	0.0	57.1
B & T publications	0.0	0.0	28.6	0.0	71.4
Ingram publications	0.0	0.0	28.6	0.0	71.4
Brodart publication	0.0	0.0	14.3	0.0	85.7

Bowker BIP
outserts 0.0 0.0 14.3 0.0 85.7
<- - - Row percents sum to 100.0% - - ->
(Average Base = 7)

25b. How effective are each of the following publications as a SPACE ADVERTISING VEHICLE?

Publication As SPACE ADVERTISING VEHICLE

	Very Effective				Not at All Effective
Library Journal	11.1%	22.2%	11.1%	22.2%	33.3%
School LJ	12.5	25.0	0.0	0.0	62.5
Choice	0.0	25.0	0.0	12.5	62.5
Booklist/RBB	25.0	0.0	0.0	25.0	50.0
American Libraries	0.0	0.0	25.0	37.5	37.5
Publishers Weekly	0.0	12.5	12.5	37.5	37.5
Billboard	0.0	0.0	12.5	12.5	75.0
Audiofile	0.0	0.0	0.0	25.0	75.0
NYT/NYT Book Review	12.5	0.0	12.5	12.5	62.5
RQ	0.0	0.0	12.5	25.0	62.5
Information Today	0.0	12.5	12.5	12.5	62.5
Booklinks	0.0	0.0	12.5	12.5	75.0
Librarian's Yellow Pages	0.0	0.0	25.0	25.0	50.0
Horn Book	0.0	12.5	25.0	12.5	50.0
VOYA	0.0	0.0	25.0	12.5	62.5
Against the Grain	22.2	22.2	0.0	0.0	55.6
Web sites:					
Bookwire	0.0	0.0	0.0	0.0	100.0
Amazon.com	11.1	0.0	0.0	22.2	66.7
B & N Web site	0.0	0.0	0.0	12.5	87.5
Rettig on Reference	0.0	12.5	12.5	0.0	75.0
B & T publications	12.5	0.0	0.0	0.0	87.5

Ingram publications	12.5	0.0	0.0	0.0	87.5
Brodart publication	12.5	0.0	0.0	0.0	87.5
Bowker BIP outserts	0.0	0.0	0.0	12.5	87.5

<--- Row percents sum to 100.0% --->
(Average Base = 8)

25c. Please specify other publication.
   Other = Regional SLA chapter newsletters

26. Do you currently sell to consortia or library purchasing groups?

   Yes   75.0%
   No   25.0% (SKIP TO Q.31)
                            Total: 100.0%
                            Base: 12

27a. Do you have sales/marketing staff devoted to working with consortia or library purchasing groups?

   Yes   55.6%
   No   44.4% (SKIP TO Q.28)
                            Total: 100.0%
                            Base: 9

(IF "YES"):
   b. What are the title(s) of these sales/marketing staff:

      1. Senior Regional Sales Manager
      2. Manager, Consortium Sales
      3. Sales Representative
      4. Sales Representative
      5. Machine Manager
      6. Vice President, Sales
      (Only Responses Given)

28. What percentage of your sales is generated by consortia or library purchasing groups?

      5 percent   42.9%

Vendor Questionnaire

7 percent	14.3%
10 percent	42.9%
Total:	100.0%
Base:	7

29. If you offer discounts to consortia, please indicate the *most* common method of discounting:

Lower per–FTE	0.0%
Volume discounts with sliding scale discount	33.3%
Flat-rate discount	66.7%
Do not offer discounts to consortia	0.0%
Total:	100.0%
Base:	9

30. What impact have consortial or library purchasing groups had on your overall sales $ volume?

Positive impact	33.3%
Negative impact	0.0%
Not sure	66.7%
Total:	100.0%
Base:	9

31. How important will consortia and library purchasing groups be to your business in the next three to five years?

Very important	30.0%
Moderately important	20.0%
Somewhat important	40.0%
Not at all important	10.0%
Total:	100.0%
Base:	10

32. For each type of library, what is the cumulative percentage of library orders filled within the following time frames?
    Filled within:

	14 Days	30 Days	60 Days	90 Days	120 Days
ARL library	25.0%	0.0%	75.0%	0.0%	0.0%

College/university (other than ARL)	20.0	20.0	60.0	0.0	0.0
Two-year college	25.0	25.0	50.0	0.0	0.0
Public	25.0	25.0	50.0	0.0	0.0
Special	50.0	50.0	0.0	0.0	0.0
School (K–8, 9–12)	50.0	25.0	25.0	0.0	0.0
Government	50.0	0.0	50.0	0.0	0.0

<--- Row percents sum to 100.0% --->
(Average Base = 4)

33. About what percentage of your "unfillable" orders fall into each of the following categories? (IF UNSURE, GIVE YOUR BEST ESTIMATE.)

	Average Percent
Out of print	28.2%
Out of stock	25.6%
Insufficient/incorrect information	3.4%
Publisher fails to respond	10.5%
Must order direct	5.1%
Not yet published	13.3%
Indefinitely delayed	6.1%
Operate from predefined inventory	0.1%
Title cancelled by publisher	2.7%
Other	5.0%
Total:	100.0%
Base:	10

34. For each type of library, about what percent order prepublication? (IF UNSURE, GIVE YOUR BEST ESTIMATE.)

	Average Percent
ARL library	12.5%
College/university (other than ARL)	18.3%
Two-year college	2.5%
Public	8.5%
Special	40.8%

School (K–8, 9–12)	4.2%
Government	11.5%
Other	1.7%
Total:	100.0%
Base:	6

35. For each type of library, are multiple copy purchases for the same title (per each location) increasing, decreasing, or remaining static?

	Increasing	Decreasing	Remaining Static
ARL library	0.0%	25.0%	75.0%
College/university (other than ARL)	0.0	25.0	75.0
Two-year college	0.0	12.5	87.5
Public	12.5	12.5	75.0
Special	0.0	37.5	62.5
School (K–8, 9–12)	0.0	14.3	85.7
Government	0.0	16.7	83.3

<- - - Row percents sum to 100.0% - - ->
(Average Base = 8)

36. How do you rate the usefulness of the following information in processing orders from libraries? (RATE EACH ON A SCALE FROM 1 = "Most useful" TO 5 = "Least useful.")

	Most Useful				Least Useful
ISBN	100.0%	0.0%	0.0%	0.0%	0.0%
ISSN	66.7	0.0	33.3	0.0	0.0
SAN	25.0	25.0	25.0	0.0	25.0
LCCN	0.0	66.7	0.0	0.0	33.3
SKU	0.0	100.0	0.0	0.0	0.0
Title	66.7	33.3	0.0	0.0	0.0
Author	50.0	33.3	8.3	8.3	0.0
Publisher	33.3	41.7	8.3	8.3	8.3
Edition	45.5	54.5	0.0	0.0	0.0
Binding	75.0	25.0	0.0	0.0	0.0
Price	25.0	25.0	37.5	12.5	0.0

Customer
account number   55.6   22.2   22.2   0.0   0.0
< - - - Row percents sum to 100.0% - - - >
(Average Base = 7)

37. Which of the following electronic services do you offer or receive?
(CIRCLE ALL THAT APPLY IN EACH COLUMN.)

	BISAC (Fixed or Variable)	SISAC	X12	EDIFACT	Other
Orders:					
To/from publishers	50.0%	0.0%	33.3%	16.7%	8.3%
From/to libraries	41.7%	0.0%	50.0%	41.7%	33.3%
From/to networks (e.g., OCLC)	16.7%	0.0%	33.3%	16.7%	16.7%
From/to turnkey vendors (e.g., GEAC)	50.0%	0.0%	25.0%	8.3%	8.3%
Invoices:					
To/from publishers	8.3%	0.0%	8.3%	8.3%	0.0%
From/to libraries	25.0%	0.0%	41.7%	33.3%	25.0%
From/to networks (e.g., OCLC)	16.7%	0.0%	16.7%	8.3%	0.0%
From/to turnkey vendors (e.g., GEAC)	8.3%	0.0%	16.7%	16.7%	8.3%
Information:					
To/from publishers	16.7%	0.0%	25.0%	8.3%	16.7%
From/to libraries	25.0%	0.0%	16.7%	8.3%	25.0%

From/to networks (e.g., OCLC)	8.3%	0.0%	16.7%	8.3%	16.7%
From/to turnkey vendors (e.g., GEAC)	8.3%	0.0%	8.3%	8.3%	8.3%

38a. How do you rate the following sources for accuracy of information on publisher title status? (RATE EACH SOURCE ON A SCALE FROM 1= "Most accurate" TO 5 = "Least accurate.")

	Most Accurate				Least Accurate
Announcements in journals	0.0%	44.4%	22.2%	33.3%	0.0%
Publisher reports	50.0	20.0	10.0	10.0	10.0
Publisher sales representatives	22.2	55.6	22.2	0.0	0.0
Online databases	27.3	36.4	36.4	0.0	0.0

b. How do you communicate this information to libraries? (CIRCLE ALL THAT APPLY.)

Status reports with returned orders	75.0%
Monthly (or more frequent) status reports	75.0%
Status reports on invoice	58.3%
Status reports on request	75.0%
Status available online	58.3%
Other	16.7%

38c. Other ways of communicating information to libraries.

Other = E-mail
　　　 Monthly cancellation notices; order confirmation reports; on-line database

39. Please feel free to comment further on any questions or problems that were dealt with in this questionnaire. (ATTACH AN ADDITIONAL SHEET IF NECESSARY.)

— Answers are somewhat skewed because we distribute primarily medical and scientific titles to health science libraries.

— A little confused; not sufficient options.

— Sales and marketing to libraries would benefit from closer cooperation between publishers and vendors. We need to become partners in providing our joint customers with a seamless flow of accurate, and current information using standardized vocabulary and data transmission products.

11

AAP/ALCTS Library Marketing Survey: Library Questionnaire

A. GENERAL

1. Which one of the following categories best describes your library? (CIRCLE THE CODE NUMBER OF THE APPROPRIATE ANSWER.)

ARL library	4.0%
College/university (other than ARL)	19.9%
Two-year college	12.3%
Public	39.5%
Special	2.7%
School	19.6%
Government	0.0%
Other	2.0%
Total:	100.0%
Base:	301

2. In which state is your library located?
   Responses not provided.

3. Of your total collection, what is the size of your book collection?

10,000 or less	16.8%
10,001 to 15,000	10.8%
15,001 to 25,000	13.1%
25,001 to 50,000	14.4%

50,001 to 75,000	6.9%
75,001 to 120,000	9.5%
120,001 to 250,000	13.4%
Over 250,000	<u>15.1%</u>
Total:	100.0%
Base:	305

4. What is the approximate size of your primary constituency?

500 or less	18.7%
501 to 1,000	13.4%
1,001 to 5,000	28.5%
5,001 to 20,000	20.7%
20,001 to 75,000	10.2%
Over 75,000	<u>8.5%</u>
Total:	100.0%
Base:	305

5. What is the library's total operating budget for the current year including salaries? (ROUND TO THE NEAREST WHOLE DOLLAR.)

$50,000 or less	25.8%
$50,001 to $100,000	11.5%
$100,001 to $250,000	17.4%
$250,001 to $500,000	12.5%
$500,001 to $1,000,000	11.5%
$1,000,001 to $3,000,000	11.8%
Over $3,000,000	<u>9.5%</u>
Total:	100.0%
Base:	305

6a. What is the library's budget for the purchase of all library materials for your current budget year? (97–98)
Base your response on your own fiscal year, i.e., Jan–Dec or July–June. (ROUND TO THE NEAREST WHOLE DOLLAR.)

$10,000 or less	25.3%
$10,001 to $25,000	14.1%

$25,001 to $50,000		10.8%
$50,001 to $100,000		14.1%
$100,001 to $250,000		14.1%
$250,001 to $1,000,000		13.1%
Over $1,000,000		8.5%
	Total:	100.0%
	Base:	305

b. Over the past five years has your materials budget . . .

Increased,		59.4%
Decreased, or		10.6%
Remained static?		30.0%
	Total:	100.0%
	Base:	303

c. Do you see your materials budget in the next five years as . . .

Increasing,		59.6%
Decreasing, or		5.0%
Remaining static?		35.4%
	Total:	100.0%
	Base:	302

7a. What percentage of the library's current year (97–98) budget do you estimate is/will be spent for the following categories of material? (IF UNSURE, GIVE YOUR BEST ESTIMATE.)

	Average Percent
Print monographs	44.9%
Print serials, periodicals	23.7%
Large print books	2.4%
Microforms	2.2%
Video formats	5.5%
Sound recordings	2.5%
Multimedia	2.2%
Online (locally mounted or CD–ROM)	5.4%
Online (remotely accessed)	5.8%

Other		5.4%
	Total:	100.0%
	Base:	234

7b. What percent of your library materials budget do you spend on children's/YA? (CIRCLE ONE)

None; library does not purchase children's/ YA materials	(SKIP TO Q.7d)	21.1%
10% or less		30.0%
11% to 25%		22.1%
26% to 50%		18.0%
51% to 75%		2.0%
Over 75%		6.8%
	Total:	100.0%
	Base:	294

7c. If you purchase children's/YA materials, what *dollar amount* do you spend on each of the following per year:

Print monographs

$0		30.9%
$1 to $500		14.8%
$501 to $1,000		7.8%
$1,001 to $2,000		5.8%
$2,001 to $5,000		12.3%
$5,001 to $10,000		9.9%
$10,001 to $20,000		7.4%
Over $20,000		11.1%
	Total:	100.0%
	Base:	243

Print serials, periodicals

$0	54.8%
$1 to $500	25.1%
$501 to $1,000	10.7%
$1,001 to $2,000	4.5%
$2,001 to $5,000	1.2%
$5,001 to $10,000	0.8%

$10,001 to $20,000		0.8%
Over $20,000		<u>2.1%</u>
	Total:	100.0%
	Base:	243

Large print books

$0		92.2%
$1 to $500		6.2%
$501 to $2,000		0.8%
$2,001 to $5,000		0.4%
Over $5,000		<u>0.4%</u>
	Total:	100.0%
	Base:	243

Microforms

$0		98.4%
$1 to $500		0.4%
$501 to $1,000		0.4%
$1,001 to $2,000		0.4%
$2,001 to $10,000		<u>0.4%</u>
	Total:	100.0%
	Base:	243

Video formats

$0		56.8%
$1 to $500		21.4%
$501 to $1,000		7.4%
$1,001 to $2,000		6.2%
$2,001 to $5,000		3.3%
$5,001 to $10,000		3.7%
Over $10,000		<u>1.2%</u>
	Total:	100.0%
	Base:	243

Sound recordings

$0		70.9%
$1 to $500		16.0%
$501 to $1,000		3.7%
$1,001 to $2,000		2.9%

$2,001 to $5,000	4.5%
$5,001 to $10,000	0.8%
$10,001 to $20,000	0.4%
Over $20,000	0.8%
Total:	100.0%
Base:	243

Multimedia

$0	77.7%
$1 to $500	13.6%
$501 to $1,000	2.5%
$1,001 to $2,000	3.7%
$2,001 to $5,000	2.1%
Over $5,000	0.4%
Total:	100.0%
Base:	243

Online (locally mounted or CD–ROM networked)

$0	83.4%
$1 to $500	6.6%
$501 to $1,000	2.5%
$1,001 to $2,000	2.5%
$2,001 to $5,000	2.5%
$5,001 to $10,000	2.1%
Over $10,000	0.4%
Total:	100.0%
Base:	243

Online (remotely accessed)

$0	93.1%
$1 to $500	2.5%
$501 to $1,000	1.2%
$1,001 to $2,000	1.2%
$2,001 to $5,000	0.8%
$5,001 to $10,000	0.4%
$10,001 to $20,000	0.4%
Over $20,000	0.4%
Total:	100.0%
Base:	243

7d. Of the budget categories listed in Q.7a (and Q.7c) above, for which categories is your spending most likely to increase most dramatically in the next five years? (CIRCLE ALL THAT APPLY.)

Print monographs	35.1%
Print serials, periodicals	23.6%
Large print books	7.9%
Microforms	2.6%
Video formats	22.0%
Sound recordings	19.3%
Multimedia	22.0%
Online (locally mounted or CD–ROM networked)	40.7%
Online (remotely accessed)	51.1%
Base:	305

B. RECOMMENDATION/ SELECTION/ ORDERING

8. Who in your library is responsible for each of the three major functions below. (CIRCLE ALL THAT APPLY IN EACH COLUMN.)

	Identification/ Recommendation	Selection/ Purchasing Decision	Order Placement
Head librarian	75.1%	72.5%	50.2%
Assistant librarian	24.6%	14.8%	8.2%
Acquisition or order librarian	15.7%	13.8%	31.8%
Reference librarian	32.8%	19.7%	5.6%
Heads of library departments	23.6%	18.0%	5.9%
Branch manager	12.8%	10.2%	2.6%
Bibliographer/subject specialist (subject language, et al.)	9.5%	8.2%	2.0%
Collection development librarian	15.1%	13.1%	6.6%
Adult services librarian	8.9%	4.9%	2.0%

Nonlibrary personnel (e.g., faculty, public trustees, professional clientele, etc.)	26.2%	6.2%	1.3%
Other	11.5%	5.2%	10.5%

<--- Base for above percentages = 305 --->

9a. Is your ordering process automated?

Yes		48.5% (SKIP TO Q.10a)
No		51.5%
	Total:	100.0%
	Base:	297

b. Will your ordering process be automated in the future?

Planned within one year	8.3%
Planned within three years	11.8%
No current plans for automation	79.9%
Total:	100.0%
Base:	144

10a. What percentage of your orders do you transmit:

	Percent
Electronically (e.g., EDI, e-mail)	34.4%
By mail	32.8%
By fax	12.3%
By phone	16.7%
Other	3.8%
Total:	100.0%
Base:	279

b. What percentage of your orders are sent to:

	Percent
Vendors (e.g., Baker and Taylor, BWI, Brodart, Ingram, etc.)	77.3%

Publishers		13.7%
Bookstores		5.8%
Online (electronic bookstores, publisher Web site)		1.9%
Other		1.3%
	Total:	100.0%
	Base:	282

11a. Does your library belong to one or more formal purchasing consortia or library purchasing groups?

Yes		42.5%
No		57.5% (SKIP TO Q.12a)
	Total:	100.0%
	Base:	301

b. How many groups of each type does your library belong to? (IF "NONE," ENTER "0.")

<u>Type</u>		<u>Percent</u>
Formal purchasing consortia		
None		36.2%
One		44.9%
Two		15.0%
Three		3.1%
Four or more		0.8%
	Total:	100.0%
	Base:	127
Informal library purchasing groups		
None		65.3%
One		29.9%
Two		1.6%
Three		1.6%
Four or more		1.6%
	Total:	100.0%
	Base:	127

National or regional utilities that also negotiate reduced prices for member purchases or services

None		47.3%
One		41.7%
Two		7.9%
Three		3.1%
	Total:	100.0%
	Base:	127

c. What kinds of agreements has your library made through these arrangements? (CIRCLE ALL THAT APPLY.)

Deeper publisher/vendor discounts for print acquisitions		0.8%
Deeper publisher/vendor discounts for nonprint acquisitions		50.8%
Favorable pricing for electronic products or services (CD–ROM, Internet based resources, etc.)		70.3%
Wider access to existing electronic products through favorable pricing		52.3%
Favorable pricing for print reference works		22.7%
Other		7.0%
	Base:	128

12a. What percent of your FY98 acquisitions budget will support consortial or library purchasing group efforts?

Under 10 percent		75.3%
10 to 25 percent		13.6%
Over 25 percent		11.1%
	Total:	100.0%
	Base:	235

b. By what percentage has your present budget for consortial purchases increased from its level in 1995?

Under 10 percent	76.8%
10 to 25 percent	13.4%
26 to 50 percent	4.2%
51 to 75 percent	1.9%

	Over 75 percent		3.7%
		Total:	100.0%
		Base:	216

c. In the next three to five years, how important will consortial or library purchasing groups' participation be to your overall acquisitions program?

	Very important		30.1%
	Moderately important		33.9%
	Not important		36.0%
		Total:	100.0%
		Base:	127

13a. Please rate the sales effectiveness of the following *publisher* promotional materials. (RATE EACH ON A SCALE FROM 1 = "Most effective" TO 5 = "Least effective.")

	Most Effective				Least Effective
Catalogs	34.6%	34.9%	19.1%	8.4%	3.0%
Reviews	64.2	19.0	9.3	4.1	3.4
Space advertising	1.8	13.8	23.6	30.9	29.9
Title listings	5.5	10.6	27.7	26.0	30.0
Sales calls	5.6	8.5	20.8	26.8	38.3
Flyers	8.4	22.4	33.9	20.3	15.0
Direct mail	10.7	21.7	35.2	19.6	12.8
Exhibits:					
ALA	12.2	20.3	23.2	8.9	35.4
ALA–Midwinter	7.2	13.1	21.7	10.0	48.0
PLA	6.8	14.1	15.1	9.8	54.2
SLA	5.2	8.4	11.0	8.9	66.5
AASL	5.2	7.3	12.0	8.9	66.6
ACRL	5.9	9.4	18.7	10.8	55.2
State shows	19.7	23.6	19.7	12.6	24.4
Regional shows	11.5	18.1	18.9	11.5	40.0
Charleston Conference	2.1	5.2	9.9	10.4	72.4

BookExpo America	1.6	5.9	12.8	7.4	72.3
Blanket order plans	3.3	9.3	16.7	12.6	58.1
Media coverage (publicity including TV, radio, magazine, etc.)	13.0	21.9	23.1	15.8	26.2
Telemarketing	0.4	1.7	10.0	17.5	70.4
Author appearances	9.0	23.0	22.5	14.8	30.7
Library entertainment /events	4.8	20.6	18.4	15.8	40.4
Advance readers editions	6.5	13.8	18.1	20.3	41.4
In house publications	2.7	9.1	20.1	20.1	48.0
Online catalogs and Web sites	16.1	24.8	20.7	15.7	22.7

<---- Row Percents Sum to 100.0% ---->
(Average Base = 239)

13b. From the list in Q.13a, chose the five most important *publisher promotional methods* and list them in order of importance.

METHOD	#1 Most Important Method	#2 Most Important Method	#3 Most Important Method	#4 Most Important Method	#5 Most Important Method
Catalogs	30.1%	27.7%	11.1%	9.2%	5.4%
Reviews	51.4	20.8	7.3	7.9	2.0
Space advertising	0.7	1.8	2.3	6.3	3.0
Title listings	0.0	2.6	8.0	4.6	2.5
Sales calls	2.5	3.3	3.4	5.4	8.4
Flyers	2.1	7.3	12.3	10.0	7.4
Direct mail	1.4	6.7	9.2	10.4	13.9
Exhibits: ALA	0.0	3.3	3.8	2.1	5.0
Exhibits: ALA– Midwinter	0.0	0.0	1.1	0.8	1.0

Exhibits: PLA	0.0	0.0	1.1	0.4	1.5
Exhibits: SLA	0.0	0.0	0.0	0.0	0.5
Exhibits: AASL	0.0	0.4	0.4	0.8	0.0
Exhibits: ACRL	0.0	0.0	1.1	0.8	0.0
Exhibits: State shows	2.5	3.6	7.3	7.9	5.4
Exhibits: Regional shows	0.4	1.1	2.7	3.8	3.5
Exhibits: Charleston Con.	0.0	0.4	0.4	0.0	0.5
Exhibits: BookExpo America	0.0	0.0	0.0	0.8	0.5
Blanket order plans	1.4	1.1	0.8	1.7	2.0
Media coverage	1.4	5.8	7.3	7.9	9.4
Telemarketing	0.0	0.4	0.4	0.4	1.0
Author appearances	0.4	1.8	3.4	7.1	5.4
Library entertainment/ events	0.0	1.1	1.5	1.7	2.0
Advance readers editions	0.0	0.4	0.4	2.5	3.5
In-house publications	0.0	0.7	0.0	0.8	0.5
Online catalogs/ Web sites	3.2	4.4	8.4	4.2	11.9
TOTAL OF OTHER METHODS	2.7	5.5	6.1	2.5	3.5
Column Total	100.0%	100.0%	100.0%	100.0%	100.0%

BASE	282	274	261	240	202
BLANKS	23	31	44	65	103
TOTAL	305	305	305	305	305
OTHER METHODS CITED	#1 Most Important Method	#2 Most Important Method	#3 Most Important Method	#4 Most Important Method	#5 Most Important Method
Visiting bookstores	0.4%	0.4%	0.4%	0.4%	
Patron requests	0.7	1.1			
School Library Journal	0.4				
Exhibits (general)	0.4	1.8	2.3	1.7	2.5
Faculty recommendations	0.4	0.4			
Best-sellers	0.4				0.5
Work by a popular author		0.4			
Knowledge of readers		0.4			
Hands on examination		0.4			
Majors report weekly		0.4			
On approval boxes of book		0.4			
On-hand selection			0.4		
"Common sense"			0.4		
Books in Print			0.4		
In-house display			0.4		

MLA exhibits			0.4		0.4
PSLA exhibits			0.4		
Technology Periodicals			0.4		
PLS			0.4		
Library Journal			0.4		
Selective weeding				0.4	
BASE	282	274	261	240	202

14a. Please rate the sales effectiveness of the following *vendor* promotional materials.

	Most Effective				Least Effective
Catalogs	41.7%	24.6%	16.3%	8.7%	8.7%
Reviews	49.5	22.1	14.4	6.3	7.7
Space advertising	4.1	10.2	29.8	26.1	29.8
Title listings	10.6	17.1	27.4	18.8	26.1
Sales calls	10.8	10.0	21.5	21.1	36.6
Flyers	9.0	18.0	36.5	20.0	16.5
Direct mail	9.1	24.9	26.8	20.6	18.6
Exhibits:					
ALA	15.9	15.5	20.4	9.1	39.1
ALA–Midwinter	7.4	9.9	20.2	12.3	50.2
PLA	5.8	9.9	15.2	10.5	58.6
SLA	5.5	5.5	13.2	12.1	63.7
AASL	6.0	5.5	11.5	12.1	64.9
ACRL	7.8	6.3	17.2	10.9	57.8
State shows	23.5	19.9	17.7	11.5	27.4
Regional shows	10.7	17.3	16.8	11.2	44.0
Charleston Conference	2.3	5.1	13.1	10.9	68.6
BookExpo America	2.3	5.7	12.6	6.9	72.5
Blanket order plans	7.1	10.2	13.8	12.8	56.1

Media coverage (publicity including TV, radio, magazine, etc.)	10.4	15.6	16.5	12.7	44.8
Telemarketing	0.5	3.9	11.6	15.0	69.0
Author appearances	11.9	16.2	19.0	13.3	39.6
Library entertainment/ events	6.7	15.3	20.1	14.4	43.5
Advance readers editions	8.4	11.3	16.7	15.3	48.3
In-house publications	6.5	8.0	18.6	18.1	48.6
Online catalogs and Web sites	17.1	23.6	15.7	15.7	27.8

<--- Row Percents Sum to 100.0% --->
(Average Base = 216)

14b. From the list in Q.14a, chose the five most important *vendor promotional methods* and list them in order of importance.

METHOD	#1 Most Important Method	#2 Most Important Method	#3 Most Important Method	#4 Most Important Method	#5 Most Important Method
Catalogs	30.5%	25.8%	9.1%	9.3%	5.4%
Reviews	36.7	20.6	9.1	9.7	3.8
Space advertising	0.8	1.2	4.3	1.9	2.7
Title listings	0.4	4.0	10.3	5.6	5.4
Sales calls	7.3	4.8	6.9	4.2	5.4
Flyers	1.9	5.6	12.9	9.7	7.6
Direct mail	2.7	4.8	3.8	15.3	16.3
Exhibits: ALA	1.2	3.2	4.3	4.6	2.7
Exhibits: ALA– Midwinter	0.0	0.8	1.3	1.4	0.5
Exhibits: PLA	0.0	0.0	0.0	1.4	1.1
Exhibits: SLA	0.0	0.4	0.4	0.5	0.5

Exhibits: AASL	0.0	0.4	0.4	0.9	0.0
Exhibits: ACRL	0.4	0.4	1.3	0.0	0.5
Exhibits: State shows	2.3	6.0	8.2	5.1	7.1
Exhibits: Regional shows	0.4	2.0	3.4	3.2	4.9
Exhibits: Charleston Con.	0.0	0.0	0.9	0.0	1.1
Exhibits: BookExpo America	0.0	0.0	0.4	0.0	0.0
Blanket order plans	1.9	2.0	2.6	1.4	1.6
Media coverage	0.8	4.0	5.2	7.9	9.2
Telemarketing	0.0	0.0	0.9	0.0	1.1
Author appearances	1.2	1.2	3.1	2.8	1.6
Library entertainment/ events	0.4	1.6	1.3	2.3	3.3
Advance readers editions	0.4	0.8	0.4	1.9	1.6
In-house publications	0.8	0.4	1.7	1.4	2.2
Online catalogs/ Web sites	6.2	5.2	4.3	6.9	12.0
TOTAL OF OTHER METHODS	3.9	4.4	3.4	2.8	2.2
Column Total	100.0%	100.0%	100.0%	100.0%	100.0%
BASE	259	248	232	216	184
BLANKS	46	57	73	89	121

OTHER METHODS CITED	#1 Most Important Method	#2 Most Important Method	#3 Most Important Method	#4 Most Important Method	#5 Most Important Method
TOTAL	305	305	305	305	305
Samples	0.4%				
"Recommended" lists	0.4	0.4			
Exhibits	0.8	2.4	1.7	1.9	1.6
Visiting bookstores	0.4		0.4		
B & T publications	0.4				
Hands on examination	0.4				
LJ Sourcebook	0.4				
Prepub offers	0.4			0.5	
Faculty recommendations	0.4				
Requests		0.4			
ACL Conference		0.4			
Special promotions		0.4			
On approval books		0.4			
On-hand selection			0.4		
WLMA Conference			0.4		
MLA Conference			0.4		0.5
Custom publications				0.5	
BASE	259	248	232	216	184

15. Is promotional material received by your library addressed to the most appropriate person or position?

Yes	53.1%
Sometimes	44.9%
No	2.0%
Total:	100.0%
Base:	301

16. How useful to you are the following types of mailings from publishers or vendors? (RATE EACH ON A SCALE FROM 1 = "Very useful" TO 5 = "Not at all useful.")

	Very Useful				Not at All Useful
Flyers	20.6%	28.2%	28.5%	11.7%	11.0%
Forthcoming announcements	27.9	27.8	26.8	9.1	8.4
Complete catalogs	48.3	23.6	16.4	8.2	3.4
Subject catalogs	38.9	31.3	20.5	5.9	3.5
Selection/ordering tools	23.0	28.1	24.5	10.2	14.2

< - - - Row Percents Sum to 100.0% - - - >
(Average Base = 286)

17. When do you prefer to receive catalogs?

	Prefer Most				Prefer Least
Fall	50.8%	16.9%	18.5%	6.3%	7.4%
Winter	13.9	33.5	32.9	5.8	13.9
Spring	21.7	25.5	26.6	9.8	16.3
Summer	14.7	15.3	27.7	8.5	33.9
Every quarter	39.2	13.9	17.5	10.3	19.1
Every month	25.7	7.1	13.1	12.6	41.5
No Preferences	22.6%				

< - - - Row Percents Sum to 100.0% - - - >
(Average Base = 183)

18. How long before titles are published do you prefer to receive selection information from publishers and/or vendors?

Six months before		7.9%
Three months before		45.0%
One month before		28.5%
At publication date		14.1%
Postpublication		4.5%
	Total:	100.0%
	Base:	291

19. How often are each of the following *information sources* used for book selection?

	Always	Often	Sometimes	Rarely	Never
Library review media (e.g., *Library Journal*, *Choice*)	50.4%	30.1%	9.6%	6.5%	3.4%
General book trade review media (e.g., *Publishers Weekly*)	21.1	25.6	22.8	18.2	12.3
Newspaper book reviews (e.g., *New York Times*)	17.4	27.9	34.5	13.2	7.0
Journal of professional disciplines (e.g., *AHA Review*)	8.0	19.3	24.8	24.5	23.4
General interest magazines (e.g., *Harper's*, *Time*)	1.8	13.6	44.1	26.9	13.6
Publisher's catalogs and promotional Literature	18.1	37.2	33.1	9.9	1.7
Vendor selection tools and promotional Literature	15.1	30.9	31.6	16.1	6.3
Bibliographic tools such as CBI, BIP,					

MARC, and vendor database	5.8	15.6	27.3	25.1	26.2
Bibliographic utility (e.g., OCLC, RLIN, WLN, etc.)	3.3	11.0	24.2	24.9	36.6
Media coverage (TV, radio, newspaper)	6.1	20.8	39.4	22.6	11.1
Internet (e.g., Bookwire)	5.0	15.3	35.5	21.9	22.3

<--- Row Percents Sum to 100.0% --->
(Average Base = 279)

20. How often are each of the following used in making a *decision to purchase* a recently published book (assuming funds are available)?

	Always	Often	Sometimes	Rarely	Never
Reviews	38.6%	44.1%	12.8%	2.8%	1.7%
Literary quality (style, readability)	21.0	51.4	18.8	6.6	2.2
Faculty requests	34.6	36.2	11.0	2.8	15.4
Student requests	16.3	34.7	31.5	6.2	11.3
Patron requests	22.8	43.9	24.3	6.4	2.6
Bargain price (good discount)	6.8	27.0	44.6	17.3	4.3
Authority of the author	20.4	54.6	21.1	2.5	1.4
Reputation of the publisher	8.3	42.8	30.2	14.7	4.0
Inclusion on recommended book list (ALA Book List etc.)	14.9	53.9	23.8	4.6	2.8
Covers a subject or area not previously represented in library	22.5	42.6	26.8	6.0	2.1
Is an important new work on a well-covered subject	21.7	42.1	27.5	6.5	2.2
Personal contact by vendor's or publisher's sales representative	1.8	11.2	31.8	37.9	17.3

Information obtained at conference exhibits	3.6	18.5	44.2	20.7	13.0
Media coverage (TV, radio, newspaper, etc.)	4.7	21.6	38.8	21.2	13.7

<--- Row Percents Sum to 100.0% --->
(Average Base = 292)

21a. How effective are each of the following publications as a REVIEW SOURCE (to spur library sales)?

Publication As REVIEW SOURCE

	Very Effective				Not at All Effective
Library Journal	60.7%	24.2%	8.3%	2.0%	4.8%
School LJ	50.5	15.5	8.0	4.3	21.9
Choice	52.3	10.2	10.8	10.2	16.5
Booklist/RBB	55.4	20.6	10.5	3.9	9.6
American Libraries	19.4	21.4	26.9	13.9	18.4
Publishers Weekly	34.6	23.3	21.3	7.9	12.9
Billboard	6.7	6.7	20.9	17.2	48.5
Audiofile	4.8	5.6	20.2	19.4	50.0
NYT/NYT Book Review	31.1	28.0	19.3	10.6	11.0
RQ	17.7	15.6	15.6	12.1	39.0
Information Today	4.2	9.3	12.7	19.5	54.3
Booklinks	11.4	9.1	25.8	11.4	42.3
Librarian's Yellow Pages	3.6	6.5	16.5	20.9	52.5
Horn Book	19.7	16.4	19.1	12.5	32.3
VOYA	19.4	12.7	14.9	9.7	43.3
Against the Grain	3.4	4.3	17.1	10.3	64.9
Web sites:					
Bookwire	6.3	13.3	22.7	14.8	42.9
Amazon.com	18.5	26.3	24.9	9.8	20.5
B & N Web site	16.0	20.2	24.5	11.7	27.6
Rettig on Reference	5.7	11.5	18.9	9.8	54.1

B & T publications	17.3	16.2	28.8	15.7	22.0
Ingram publications	16.3	17.5	18.1	13.8	34.3
Brodart publication	11.9	13.9	17.9	18.5	37.8
Bowker BIP outserts	3.6	5.8	18.1	23.9	48.6

<- - - - Row percents sum to 100.0% - - - >
(Average Base = 163)

21b. How effective are each of the following publications as a SPACE ADVERTISING VEHICLE?

Publication As SPACE ADVERTISING VEHICLE

	Very Effective				Not at All Effective
Library Journal	29.1%	20.7%	28.5%	9.8%	11.9%
School LJ	19.0	17.0	24.2	11.1	28.7
Choice	25.2	16.5	13.7	17.3	27.3
Booklist/RBB	22.2	21.0	26.2	13.6	17.0
American Libraries	14.0	17.5	30.4	19.3	18.7
Publishers Weekly	22.8	19.9	24.1	13.3	19.9
Billboard	8.5	3.4	16.9	18.6	52.6
Audiofile	1.8	4.6	22.0	18.3	53.3
NYT/NYT Book Review	22.3	21.1	23.4	14.9	18.3
RQ	6.7	13.3	18.3	18.3	43.4
Information Today	1.9	4.9	14.6	19.4	59.2
Booklinks	7.0	7.9	21.9	16.7	46.5
Librarian's Yellow Pages	6.3	10.2	18.1	12.6	52.8
Horn Book	7.1	14.2	18.9	20.5	39.3
VOYA	3.4	10.3	18.8	17.9	49.6
Against the Grain	2.9	2.9	16.5	10.7	67.0
Web sites:					
Bookwire	7.1	8.8	21.2	15.0	47.7
Amazon.com	21.6	16.0	21.0	14.8	26.6
B & N Web site	13.3	20.0	20.7	14.8	31.2
Rettig on Reference	3.0	4.0	16.8	11.9	64.3
B & T publications	16.5	17.1	23.8	15.9	26.7

Ingram publications	15.9	10.9	25.4	11.6	36.2
Brodart publication	12.1	12.1	17.4	15.2	43.2
Bowker BIP outserts	7.3	4.1	14.6	21.1	52.7

<----- Row percents sum to 100.0% ----->
(Average Base = 137)

22. How important are each of the following when making purchasing decisions from publishers and vendors? (RATE EACH ON A SCALE FROM 1 = "Very important" TO 5 = "Not at all important.")

	Very Important				Not at All Important
Price	44.0%	34.4%	16.5%	3.4%	1.7%
Discount	50.8	31.1	12.5	2.8	2.8
Reviews	63.1	26.0	7.0	2.5	1.4
Reputation of author	45.0	42.5	10.3	1.8	0.4
Inclusion on recommended lists and awards	37.7	40.2	15.9	4.0	2.2
Media coverage	7.0	20.7	34.0	25.8	12.5
Web site, online publicity and information	4.9	13.6	30.7	25.0	25.8
Author tours	2.7	12.2	22.1	28.8	34.2
Binding quality	19.6	33.9	28.8	8.5	9.2
Binding type	16.1	32.6	29.6	13.1	8.6
Acid free paper	10.4	27.1	29.1	17.8	15.6
Bibliographic tools like CIP, BIP	9.1	22.4	32.8	16.7	19.0
Overall reputation of publisher or imprint	14.8	43.2	26.1	9.5	6.4
Content	69.1	21.8	5.8	1.1	2.2
Free freight	21.9	27.7	28.9	10.6	10.9
Customer service	33.8	36.7	19.3	6.2	4.0
On-time shipping with adequate packing standards	31.7	36.9	22.4	4.5	4.5

EDI capability	5.1	14.8	31.9	18.1	30.1
Toll-free 800 numbers	29.7	25.7	21.4	12.7	10.5
Telemarketing	0.8	2.3	9.2	23.4	64.3
Sales representatives	5.3	13.5	25.2	24.1	31.9
Availability of standing orders	12.3	20.5	23.1	18.3	25.8
Preprocessing services	9.8	19.2	18.1	14.3	38.6
Promotional materials	2.7	11.0	30.7	27.8	27.8
Direct mail	6.1	11.1	30.3	26.1	26.4

<--- Row Percents Sum to 100.0% --->
(Average Base = 269)

23. Do you have a written selection policy statement?

Yes		81.1%
No		18.9%
	Total:	100.0%
	Base:	269

24. What percentage of your materials purchases are multiple copies?

1 to 10 percent		87.5%
11 to 20 percent		5.4%
21 to 30 percent		3.4%
31 to 40 percent		1.0%
41 to 50 percent		0.0%
More than 50 percent		2.7%
	Total:	100.0%
	Base:	294

25. When a title is published in more than one format, which ones would your library normally prefer to buy? Choose up to five formats; number below in order of preference (1 = *most preferred*).

	Most	2nd Most
Hardcover	78.8%	10.5%
Paperback	14.2	48.8
Large print	1.4	10.2
Video formats	0.6	5.2

Microform	0.6	0.0
Audio (spoken word)	0.6	10.2
CD–ROM (multimedia)	0.3	2.6
Online (locally mounted)	1.6	1.6
Online (remotely accessed)	1.6	4.3
Other	0.3	0.0
No second preference		6.6
Total:	100.0%	100.0%
Base:	305	305

26. What percentage of your materials budget is spent for backlist materials? (CIRCLE ONE ANSWER IN EACH COLUMN.)

	Book	Nonbook
None	15.1%	39.6%
1 to 10 percent	63.6	50.8
11 to 20 percent	16.5	4.8
21 to 30 percent	2.7	2.4
31 to 40 percent	1.0	0.8
41 to 50 percent	0.3	0.8
51 to 75 percent	0.3	0.0
More than 75 percent	0.3	0.8
Total:	100.0%	100.0%
Base:	291	248

27. What prompts backlist ordering? (CIRCLE ALL THAT APPLY.)

Replacement copies	83.3%
Patron requests	65.6%
New courses	31.1%
New departments/programs	25.2%
Research projects	20.7%
Grants, special funds, etc.	22.3%
Other	7.9%
Base:	305

28. How often is each of the following information sources used for backlist purchasing?

	Always	Frequently	Sometimes	Rarely	Never
Publisher's catalogs	18.5%	32.3%	29.8%	9.3%	10.1%
Book dealer's catalogs	10.7	20.2	29.2	17.6	22.3
Foreign bibliographies	1.4	2.8	8.5	26.5	60.8
Scholarly journals	5.1	8.8	24.7	23.3	38.1
Books in Print	26.9	35.8	20.1	5.2	12.0
Book Review Digest	3.2	9.6	24.3	25.7	37.2
Essay and General Literature Index	1.4	5.2	13.1	25.8	54.5
Library of Congress catalogs including NUC	1.9	4.3	10.0	24.2	59.6
Guide to Reprints	0.9	5.7	9.9	20.3	63.2
Guide to Microforms in Print	0.9	5.2	8.0	19.2	66.7
Reprint Review Bulletin	0.0	2.0	5.9	17.6	74.5
Bibliographic utility (OCLC,RLIN)	8.0	15.1	19.8	14.6	42.5
Vendor selection list	7.0	19.4	27.8	16.7	29.1
Vendor electronic database	9.9	20.7	22.5	10.4	36.5
Internet (e.g., Antiquarian or other online bookstores)	9.6	25.8	22.7	14.0	27.9

<---- Row Percents Sum to 100.0% ---->
(Average Base = 221)

29. Are reprints purchased?

Frequently		7.7%
Sometimes		81.2%
Never		11.1%
	Total:	100.0%
	Base:	298

30. Is it important to have the bibliographic data of the original publication in promotional materials?

Yes	74.0%
No	26.0%
Total:	100.0%
Base:	292

31. How frequently do you place firm orders for library materials?

Daily (almost continually)	19.7%
Weekly	20.0%
Biweekly	12.9%
Monthly	17.6%
Twice a year	4.7%
Once a fiscal year	1.7%
Irregularly (when need arises or time permits)	20.3%
Other	3.1%
Total:	100.0%
Base:	295

32a. What percentage of the book material purchased annually is preprocessed (e.g., catalog card, pocket, etc.)? (CIRCLE ONE ANSWER IN EACH COLUMN IF APPLICABLE.)

	Physical Preprocessing Only	Cataloging Data
None	62.0%	59.3%
1 to 10 percent	8.7	10.6
11 to 20 percent	3.1	1.5
21 to 30 percent	4.5	3.3
31 to 40 percent	3.1	1.8
41 to 50 percent	2.4	2.6
More than 50 percent	16.2	20.9
Total:	100.0%	100.0%
Base:	286	273

b. What percentage of *non*book materials purchased annually (including multimedia) are preprocessed? (CIRCLE ONE ANSWER IN EACH COLUMN IF APPLICABLE.)

	Physical Preprocessing Only	Cataloging Data
None	84.4%	80.9%
10 percent or less	9.1	9.2
11 to 20 percent	1.7	1.8
21 to 30 percent	1.0	1.8
31 to 40 percent	0.0	0.7
41 to 50 percent	1.0	1.1
More than 50 percent	2.8	4.4
Total:	100.0%	100.0%
Base:	286	271

33a. Does your library participate in any plan or arrangement that allows materials to be sent without a specific order being issued (e.g., blanket orders, approval plans, leasing?)

Yes	47.3%
No	52.7% (SKIP TO Q.34)
Total:	100.0%
Base:	298

b. With which of the following does your library have such arrangements? (CIRCLE ALL THAT APPLY.)

Publishers only	22.0%
Vendor only	29.8%
Publishers and vendors	48.8%
Other	1.4%
Base:	141

c. What percentage of your book materials are purchased through such arrangements?

10 percent or less	52.1%
11 to 20 percent	22.1%
21 to 30 percent	10.7%
31 to 40 percent	4.3%
41 to 50 percent	2.9%

More than 50 percent 7.9%
Total: 100.0%
Base: 140

d. What percentage of your nonbook materials, including multimedia, are purchased through such arrangements?

10 percent or less	81.2%
11 to 20 percent	11.3%
21 to 30 percent	3.8%
31 to 40 percent	0.8%
41 to 50 percent	0.8%
More than 50 percent	2.3%
Total:	100.0%
Base:	133

34. About what percentage of your annual materials budget do you spend with:

	Percent
Publishers directly	22.2%
Vendors directly	74.7%
Other	3.1%
Total:	100.0%
Base:	268

35a. How often do the following factors determine or influence your decision to order direct from *publishers*? (RATE EACH ON A SCALE FROM 1 = "Usually" TO 5 = "Never.")

	Usually				Never
Publisher prepublication offers	31.2%	25.4%	20.2%	11.4%	11.8%
Publishers' direct only policy	48.3	16.3	12.2	9.5	13.7
Bidding or contractual requirement	3.3	5.3	6.5	15.1	69.8
Geographic proximity	1.6	6.9	11.8	22.0	57.7
Free freight	20.0	18.5	21.9	17.7	21.9
Return policy	20.0	21.9	20.0	13.5	24.6
Discounts	42.3	27.7	12.8	5.5	11.7

Systems tie-in	4.7	3.9	9.4	20.6	61.4
Past performance	22.6	25.7	22.2	9.7	19.8
Speed of delivery	20.2	28.3	22.9	8.1	20.5
Packaging	6.5	10.9	26.2	21.8	34.6
Sales representative	5.9	12.2	25.6	18.5	37.8
Availability of standing orders	13.2	14.0	19.6	16.8	36.4
Preprocessing services	3.3	11.8	11.4	13.9	59.6
Special invoicing or billing service	4.9	10.2	22.8	16.3	45.8
Fill rate	16.5	23.0	24.2	8.1	28.2
Customer service	25.7	23.4	23.5	6.2	21.2
Reputation	18.4	23.6	27.6	8.4	22.0
Peer recommendation	9.3	20.6	26.2	14.5	29.4

<--- Row Percents Sum to 100.0% --->
(Average Base = 254)

35b: From the list in Q.35a, choose the *five most influential factors* that affect your decision to order from a *publisher*.

FACTOR	#1 Most Important Factor	#2 Most Important Factor	#3 Most Important Factor	#4 Most Important Factor	#5 Most Important Factor
Publisher prepub. offers	20.8%	18.3%	11.1%	4.8%	3.7%
Publishers direct only policy	27.7	12.6	4.4	6.3	2.1
Bidding or contract req.	1.2	0.4	2.2	0.5	1.1
Geographic proximity	0.0	0.4	1.3	0.5	2.1
Free freight	1.9	7.3	10.2	8.7	4.2
Return policy	0.8	5.7	7.1	4.8	10.5
Discounts	23.1	22.0	16.0	8.7	4.2
Systems tie-in	0.0	0.4	0.0	0.0	0.0
Past performance	4.6	2.4	7.1	9.1	10.0

166   Chapter 11

Speed of delivery	1.9	8.5	6.7	12.5	12.1
Packaging	0.0	0.0	0.4	1.0	2.1
Sales rep.	1.2	2.4	3.6	1.4	2.1
Avail. of standing orders	3.1	4.5	4.0	4.3	4.7
Preprocessing services	0.0	0.4	2.7	2.4	2.6
Special invoice/ billing svs.	0.4	0.0	3.1	2.9	0.5
Fill rate	4.6	4.1	4.9	8.7	6.3
Customer service	4.2	5.7	9.3	10.1	14.7
Reputation	1.2	4.1	?.?	7.?	10.5
Peer recommend- ation	0.8	0.8	2.2	4.8	5.8
TOTAL OF OTHER FACTORS	2.7	0.0	1.3	1.4	0.5
Column Total	100.0%	100.0%	100.0%	100.0%	100.0%
BASE	260	246	225	208	190
BLANKS	45	59	80	97	115
TOTAL	305	305	305	305	305

OTHER FACTORS LISTED	#1 Most Important Factor	#2 Most Important Factor	#3 Most Important Factor	#4 Most Important Factor	#5 Most Important Factor
Price	1.2				
Required by publishers	0.4				
Specialty books	0.4				
Not available through vendors	0.4				
Other	0.4			0.4	
Ease of ordering					

Binding		0.4			
Sole service		0.4			
Current and up to date		0.4		0.4	
Local source				0.4	
Patron fiction interest					0.5
BASE	253	248	238	213	197

36a. How often do the following factors influence your decision to order from *a vendor*?

	Usually				Never
Bidding or contractual requirement	16.3%	7.5%	12.3%	13.5%	50.4%
Geographic proximity	5.2	9.2	19.2	20.8	45.6
Free freight	36.3	29.2	15.4	8.2	10.9
Return policy	38.5	29.8	18.1	6.8	6.8
Discounts	69.1	22.5	5.8	1.1	1.5
Systems tie-in	12.3	11.5	17.0	17.4	41.8
Past performance	48.7	29.0	12.6	4.5	5.2
Speed of delivery	44.5	30.7	14.8	4.4	5.6
Packaging	13.0	20.6	32.8	17.0	16.6
Sales representative	10.8	17.4	28.5	17.0	26.3
Availability of standing orders	18.9	20.1	17.3	15.7	28.0
Preprocessing services	17.5	17.5	10.0	11.6	43.4
Special invoicing or billing service	14.1	18.5	22.2	19.4	25.8
Fill rate	42.3	26.9	15.4	5.4	10.0
Customer service	47.1	29.4	15.1	2.9	5.5
Reputation	35.3	32.2	22.0	3.1	7.5
Peer recommendation	16.5	22.2	28.7	14.9	17.7

<- - - - Row percents sum to 100.0% - - - >
(Average Base = 258)

36b. From the list in Q.36a, chose the *five most influential factors* that affect your decision to order from a *vendor*.

FACTOR	#1 Most Important Factor	#2 Most Important Factor	#3 Most Important Factor	#4 Most Important Factor	#5 Most Important Factor
Bidding or contract req.	9.9%	0.4%	0.4%	0.9	2.0
Geographic proximity	0.4	0.0	0.4	0.9	1.0
Free freight	4.3	14.1	10.5	8.5	7.6
Return policy	1.2	7.7	9.2	13.1	10.2
Discounts	46.2	21.8	11.3	8.5	2.5
Systems tie-in	2.0	2.4	1.3	0.9	1.0
Past performance	7.9	5.7	7.1	12.7	7.6
Speed of delivery	3.2	8.9	13.9	14.1	15.2
Packaging	0.0	0.4	0.0	0.9	0.5
Sales rep.	2.4	1.2	1.7	3.8	2.0
Avail. of standing orders	1.6	0.8	2.5	4.2	4.0
Preprocessing services	2.4	4.4	5.9	2.3	3.6
Special invoice/ billing svs.	0.8	2.4	1.7	1.9	1.5
Fill rate	7.1	14.5	17.6	4.2	9.6
Customer service	5.1	10.5	11.3	17.8	18.8
Reputation	2.0	2.0	3.4	2.8	9.6
Peer recommendation	0.8	1.6	0.8	1.9	2.5
TOTAL OF OTHER FACTORS	2.8	1.2	0.8	0.5	0.5
Column Total	100.0%	100.0%	100.0%	100.0%	100.0%
BASE	253	248	238	213	197
BLANKS	52	57	67	92	108
TOTAL	305	305	305	305	305

OTHER FACTORS LISTED	#1 Most Important Factor	#2 Most Important Factor	#3 Most Important Factor	#4 Most Important Factor	#5 Most Important Factor
Ease of ordering	0.4				
Regular selection	0.4				
Direct only policy	0.4				
Has own specialty	0.4				
Historical relationship	0.4				
Need/use	0.4				
Convenience	0.4				
Catalog available		0.4			
Less P.O.s		0.4			
One-stop shopping		0.4			
Book selection			0.4		
Format			0.4		
Local source				0.5	
Lower price					0.5
BASE	253	248	238	213	197

37a. Is there a dollar amount for an individual item that will cause the acquisition decision process to change? (e.g., if an item costs more than $100 then the decision to acquire must be made at a higher level.)

  Yes   29.1%
  No   <u>70.9%</u> (SKIP TO Q.38a)
        Total: 100.0%
        Base: 289

b. What is the dollar amount?

$50 or less 28.6%
$51 to $100 22.6%
$101 to $250 23.8%
Over $250 25.0%
Total: 100.0%
Base: 84

38a. Are there factors other than dollar amount that will cause a change in the acquisition decision process?

Yes 37.5%
No 62.5% (SKIP TO Q.39a)
Total: 100.0%
Base: 277

b. Please explain: *SEE ATTACHED REPORT FOR ANSWERS TO OPEN ENDED QUESTION 38B*

39a. If the selection involves electronic material, would the acquisition process differ?
THE RESPONSE CATEGORIES FOR QUESTION 39A (YES/NO) WERE OMITTED FROM THE FINAL PRINTED COPY OF THE LIBRARY SURVEY

b. Please explain: *SEE ATTACHED REPORT FOR ANSWERS TO OPEN ENDED QUESTION 39B*

40. How often do the following factors lead to making the decision NOT to purchase a title? (CIRCLE 5 = "Not applicable" IF NEVER A FACTOR.)

	Always	Frequently	Sometimes	Rarely	Not Applicable
Available in other formats	1.1%	12.9%	43.8%	29.7%	12.5%
Available in other libraries	3.6	16.7	45.6	26.1	8.0

Lack of funds	35.9	33.1	22.3	7.7	1.0
Physical characteristics	4.5	15.5	48.6	21.6	9.8
Not on acid free paper	1.9	5.7	19.4	46.8	26.2
Lack of cataloging in publication (CIP) data	1.9	2.7	13.1	43.5	38.8
Controversial content	3.4	9.2	32.8	39.7	14.9
Out of print (OP)	29.7	28.9	24.6	10.4	6.4
Out of stock (OS)	13.5	28.7	38.2	13.1	6.5
Outside of collection scope	28.9	26.6	23.2	13.1	8.2
Price too high	18.8	36.1	35.7	6.5	2.9
Reputation of the publisher	6.1	16.0	40.6	27.8	9.5
Nonreturnable	15.0	14.7	33.5	24.8	12.0
Requires prepayment	17.0	12.1	27.2	31.2	12.5

<---- Row percents sum to 100.0% ---->
(Average Base = 270)

41. What type of materials do you usually order before their publication? (CIRCLE ALL THAT APPLY.)

Popular	45.2%
Technical	9.8%
Reference	59.7%
Reprints	5.2%
Other	3.6%

Base: 305

C. CUSTOMER SERVICE

42. Are you satisfied with the quality of reporting for materials on order from the following?

	a. Accuracy				b. Timeliness			
	Yes	No	Total	Base	Yes	No	Total	Base
Publishers	87.9%	12.1%	100.0%	265	79.2%	20.8%	100.0%	250
Vendors	92.4%	7.6%	100.0%	278	90.0%	9.1%	100.0%	265

43. How often are materials on order reported as unavailable?

	Always	Frequently	Sometimes	Rarely	Never
Print monographs	1.1%	13.9%	63.9%	19.3%	1.8%
Print serials, periodicals	0.8	5.3	31.6	51.8	10.5
Large print books	1.2	6.4	39.8	36.4	16.2
Microforms	1.2	2.3	21.1	45.6	29.8
Video formats	0.9	7.6	46.1	34.7	10.7
Sound recordings	1.0	5.2	42.8	40.1	10.9
Multimedia	1.1	2.8	33.0	46.9	16.2
Online (locally mounted or CD–ROM networked)	1.2	2.3	14.0	49.8	32.7
Online (remotely accessed)	1.3	2.5	16.6	43.3	36.3

⟵ Row Percents Sum to 100.0% - - - ⟶
(Average Base = 199)

44. What do you usually do when items are NOT available?

Hold and submit later	26.3%
Switch resources	17.2%
Request title on ILL	3.7%
Cancel order	24.6%
Other (SPECIFY)	<u>28.2%</u>
Total:	100.0%
Base:	297

45. Rate the reasons why you have returned materials.

	Most Frequent				Least Frequent
Defective product	50.4%	18.6%	13.6%	9.4%	8.0%
Shipping damage	27.9	21.1	18.2	21.5	11.3
Duplicate shipment by publisher/ vendor	20.0	21.5	23.0	19.6	15.9
Picking errors	11.3	13.3	23.4	28.6	23.4
Price increase	2.7	3.9	13.2	38.7	41.5

Wrong item sent	25.9	20.8	21.5	22.3	9.5
Wrong shipping address	6.3	3.5	10.6	28.2	51.4
Approval plan	8.8	8.8	15.9	17.5	49.0
Wrong title ordered	6.1	11.5	24.8	34.7	22.9
Inappropriate material	4.2	7.7	12.6	31.1	44.4
Duplicate order by library	11.6	15.0	25.5	30.7	17.2
Incorrect processing	2.8	3.6	8.4	22.4	62.8

<- - - - Row percents sum to 100.0% - - - >
(Average Base = 264)

46. How often do publishers representatives visit you?

Frequently		5.1%
Sometimes		72.1%
Never		<u>22.8%</u> (SKIP TO Q.48a)
	Total:	100.0%
	Base:	294

47a. What do you expect publishers representatives to do for you? (CIRCLE ALL THAT APPLY.)

Present new titles		80.7%
Present backlist titles		28.2%
Place orders		27.3%
Troubleshoot problems		53.4%
Provide special services		23.5%
Discuss special services		39.9%
Discuss market research		10.5%
Discuss publishing trends		21.4%
Other		4.2%
	Base:	238

b. How useful are their visits?

Very useful	9.7%
Moderately useful	30.5%

Somewhat useful		42.5%
Not at all useful		17.3%
	Total:	100.0%
	Base:	226

48a. How often does your library receive telemarketing calls (offer of materials for sale by telephone) from *publishers*?

Frequently		53.2%
Sometimes		41.7%
Never		5.1% (SKIP TO Q.49a)
	Total:	100.0%
	Base:	295

b. How useful are these telemarketing calls?

Very useful		0.0%
Moderately useful		6.4%
Somewhat useful		29.5%
Not at all useful		64.1%
	Total:	100.0%
	Base:	281

49a. How often do the representatives of vendors visit you?

Frequently		8.1%
Sometimes		73.1%
Never		18.8% (SKIP TO Q.50a)
	Total:	100.0%
	Base:	298

b. What do you expect from these representatives? (CIRCLE ALL THAT APPLY.)

Present new titles	50.0%
Present backlist titles	18.2%
Assist in placing orders	33.1%
Troubleshoot problems	71.9%
Provide special services	36.8%
Discuss special services	56.6%

Discuss market research	9.5%
Discuss publishing trends	20.7%
Introduce new services	65.7%
Train on electronic products	40.5%
Other	2.1%
Base:	250

c. How useful are their visits?

Very useful		18.5%
Moderately useful		35.6%
Somewhat useful		38.6%
Not at all useful		7.3%
	Total:	100.0%
	Base:	233

50a. How often does your library receive telemarketing calls (offer of materials for sale by telephone) from *vendors*?

Frequently		23.5%
Sometimes		46.2%
Never		30.3% (SKIP TO Q.51a)
	Total:	100.0%
	Base:	294

b. How useful are these telemarketing calls?

Very useful		1.0%
Moderately useful		8.3%
Somewhat useful		38.0%
Not at all useful		52.7%
	Total:	100.0%
	Base:	205

51a. Does your library have Internet access?

Yes		94.3%
No		5.7% (SKIP TO Q.52)
	Total:	100.0%
	Base:	300

b. Can you accommodate electronic invoicing/payment?

Yes		27.1%
No		72.9%
	Total:	100.0%
	Base:	269

52. How often do you use the following when ordering?

	Usually	Sometimes	Never
International Standard Book Number (ISBN)	82.9%	13.7%	3.4%
Library of Congress Book Number (LCBN)	12.5	34.0	53.5
Standard Address Number (SAN)	5.0	14.6	80.4
International Standard Serial Number (ISSN)	31.6	33.2	35.2
Stock Keeping Units (SKU)	4.9	12.3	82.8

<- - - Row Percents Sum to 100.0% - - ->
(Average Base = 256)

53. Are you currently using or planning to use within three years

	Yes	No	Total	Base
The BISAC "fixed" computer ordering format?	13.8%	86.2%	100.0%	246
The SISAC X12 computer ordering format?	4.3%	95.7%	100.0%	233
The BISAC X-12 ordering format?	6.8%	93.2%	100.0%	235
EDIFACT?	7.0%	93.0%	100.0%	229

Open Ended Responses to Question 38b
Are there factors other than dollar amount that will cause a change in the acquisition decision process?

— Content not likely to be used in near future. Content not suitable for community.

— Some items (equipment) may require board action.

— Percentage off list price.

— Unavailability of budgeted dollars.

— We try to have the library committee make any decisions.

— Always would prefer books to be hardbound. Occasionally, only paperbound is available.

— Electronic Materials

— Quality of material—type of material.

— Multiple copies.

— Sometimes the money budgeted is taken away for "more necessary" services.

— Who requested materials.

— Need of acquisition.

— I purchase much according to curriculum needs. If a class is added or dropped, or a new teacher emphasizes different materials, then I purchase.

— Need.

— Format—CD–ROM or online. Esoteric information that may not be used widely.

— We order paperback editions when the hardcover costs more than $10 over the paper price.

— Time during fiscal year and how much remains in budget.

— All purchases must be approved by the superintendent of schools.

— Public controversy.

— Usefulness, change in curriculum.

— Decisions are based primarily on curriculum needs. If the college programs or disciplines change, it would affect the acquisition decision process. Budget reduction would also be a factor.

— Budget.

— Continuing publication; equipment or special format involved.

— Interlibrary loan—children's budget is separate but might purchase an item from general budget if comes across as an ILL request.

— Peer recommendations change decision on acquisitions, as well as, new curriculum changes and needs by teachers.

— Sufficient funds in the budget.

— Oral explanation to the principal why I think this expensive item is necessary.

— Everything I order must be approved by a group of parents, teachers, and administrators.

— Staff recommendations.

— "Type" of material. College is Seminary—"Theology." Some materials would definitely have to be reviewed and approved.

— When material is available in multiple format, e.g., hardcover vs. paper vs. audio, public services personnel may be consulted about preferred format.

— Need for collection.

— If prepayment is required, it takes longer to order.

— If collection development manager feels item might be appropriate for all branches in system she encourages all to consider it.

— Dollar level combined with whether this is a one-time expense or an on-going commitment (e.g., Subscriptions). Also, whether the title requires computer support will affect the decision process.

— Order cannot be filled before end of fiscal year or budget has been depleted before requestor made request.

— Bids go out to vendors with over $10,000 annual purchasing; sole-source allows us to skip bidding process.

— Appropriateness of request. If a faculty member orders foreign language materials at graduate level, for example.

— Duplicate copies.

— When more than one branch selects a reference title or an expensive non-fiction title, a consultation determines the number of copies for the system.

— Request for multiple copies.

— We stop acquiring when money runs out, as it always does.

— Quality of content.

— Purchase of AV equipment, computers, printers, software. If someone requests certain printer, one that I don't normally buy, I would request justification or talk it over with the principal. Also selection of software to run off server.

— Number of volumes in a set; format (e.g., electronic format)

— If you have back orders, save these until you have service or the cost of freight is more than the books.

— Ordering type of book not usually ordered.

— Type of material.

— Relevance to the curriculum.

— Faculty recommendations, curriculum needs for supporting new classes or programs, all affect purchasing, in that additional dollars may be spent on larger purchases considered.

— Memorial/gift request; content; local history

— Whether there is any money at all; also, what collection development priorities are foremost.

— If a product is too expensive—e.g., $90 for a book or video, I don't consider it—unless it is an item we have sought out for a specific need. Flyers with most items at high cost are discarded immediately.

— The needs and interests of patrons and patron requests will sometimes change the decision process.

— How much we need materials in that subject area and how difficult they are to find.

— General money problems.

— Customer service is very important.

— Request for CD–ROMs.

— Budget balance.

— We are a small library—availability of space.

— Format. Because we have limited technical support, we rarely order anything other than periodical indexes in CD–ROM format.

— Need in a particular area.

— Budget freeze.

— Return policy; discounts.

— Media and serials need extra approval.

— Limited allocation of funds.

— If one department wanted to purchase something expensive, I would ask the principal for funds.

— 1. A single request for many single items. 2. Electronic/CD–ROM requests.

— Yes—More discussion w/colleagues.

— Discount

— Addition of CD–ROMs and electronic utilities, because of licensing agreement & system configuration decisions.

— The type of item that is being ordered—usually electronic, e.g., CD–ROM or electronic access only.

— Publisher or vendor won't fill out W-9; size too small to process; doesn't fit the Collection Development Policy.

— Very scientific items; rare or out of print; foreign press items.

— If a contract or standing order is involved.

— Remote access and multimedia material require special consideration.

— Students prefer computer much more.

— Existence of multiple formats for the same item (title).

— Significant discrepancy between estimated or announced price and actual price; also format of product.

— As a recently hired head librarian my acquisition requests have received close scrutiny by the V.P. of Academics. This scrutiny is reducing over time.

— Grant requirements.

— Decline in size of program. Same or similar holdings at other CMC libraries.

— Format and binding.

— New Media—e.g., beginning a collection of Books on CD.

— For example, if a book can be purchased from a vendor or publisher.

— Change in personnel.

— If the material is out of print or needed for reserve.

— Time of year is close to or following receipt of financial aid money by the college.

— Questionable subject area so need expert advice or library committee approval.

— Interdisciplinary material, hardware requirements for online material, etc.

— Need.

— Objection of principal who signs purchase orders, or central office staff who have a question on reason for purchase.

— Format of item; general state of acquisitions budget.

—- Fill rate and speed.

— Input from affected areas, such as reference.

— Poor customer service.

— Library ID# 1269

— Availability of materials.

— Need for item, High / low priority.

— Subject matter; popularity of material, how many

— Reference works & electronic resources are selected by committee.

— Problems with a publisher or vendor—i.e., very poor fill rate.

— If board policy changed, I would comply.

— In the year prior to RFP (Requests For Proposals), we can do sample testing with vendors.

— Unusual purchases; purchasing on a consortia level.

— Format, ease of handling for circulation, binding, limited editions, CD–ROM products.

— Electronic availability.

Open Ended Responses to Question 39b
If the selection involves electronic material, would the acquisition process differ?

— Yes, some books on video with an R rating. Policy does not permit R purchases.

— Do not buy.

— Would have to show how much use is going to take place to be worth the money expended.

— Yes, review by faculty committee. Chose what they think is best for the school.

— Yes, technology committee

— All three librarians (Lib. Director, Ref. Lib., Public Service Lib.) would discuss, then decide

— Most of our CD–ROM materials are generic—encyclopedias, sirs, magazine index, etc.

— Coordination with cooperating libraries.

— Yes. Administration initiates and decides purchase. Reference may advise or request.

— Yes, library staff decision.

—- No, I do all the ordering, in whatever form.

— At this point, no, but we have no formally accepted collection development policy.

— Only if the cost is high.

— Networked products are agreed upon by a district wide peer reference group, based on common usage needs.

— Must have appropriate equipment.

— Goes for approval to different person in district.

— Electronic materials, involved technology needs, and technical requirements.

Library Questionnaire 185

— "Type" of material. College is seminary—"Theology." Some materials would definitely have to be reviewed or approved.

— Yes. Consultation with technical staff to assure compatibility with hardware and network capacity.

— Must be compatible with existing hardware/software.

— Yes—must see operate

— Yes—preview trial required

— License agreement

— Branches do all ordering from B&T. Items not available from B&T or direct from publisher items are referred to collection development manager to order.

— Dollar level combined with whether this is a one-time expense or an on-going commitment (e.g., subscription). Also, whether the title requires computer support will affect the decision process.

— Online resources are library director decisions only.

— Reviewed by assistant director.

— I do this, plus site license, but often ask opinion of business education/computer teacher, who is also a system operator.

— Acquisitions Librarian confers with most appropriate/affected librarians.

— Have to evaluate software and hardware issues, printing.

— Yes, electronic acquisitions are done only at director or tech coordinator level.

— Videos, CDs, CD–ROMS—these types of materials are somewhat limited by cost, due to their fragile state and replacement costs.

— Not dramatically.

— The process remains virtually the same, except that generally, all of the reference librarians discuss technology extensively, if the cost is high.

— Yes. Conduct a trial (hands-on) of material.

— We do not have machines to run all formats, and only purchase formats we can use.

— Yes. Can the material be purchased cheaper in print form?

— Factors such as user interface, access methods, license terms and simultaneous users would be important. Of course, pricing is most important.

— No. The money problems still rule.

— Yes. Need to investigate all kinds of issues before deciding to purchase.

— Format. Because we have limited technical support, we rarely order anything other than periodical indexes in CD-ROM format.

— We are not yet equipped to use much electronic material.

— If there are questions about networking a product or our technical ability to run a program, I would discuss it with our Technology Manager.

— More likely to do on approval ordering.

— Price would naturally be higher.

— Not really, except I would consult the technology committee for extra funds.

— Yes (see above).

— Yes—more discussion w/colleagues.

— Many more factors to consider in this format. There is no uniformity in licensing and network pricing, etc.

— This decision affects many departments and employees, and usually require specific hardware that may not be available, or requires maintenance / tech. support.

— Depending on format we may have to consult with the college's computing staff.

— Would probably involve the Library Director, especially if involves a subscription or standing order.

— Only to add; we don't purchase first run video releases.

— Yes. We have grants for health materials and now, there are venues which offer archived/accessed electronic journals. Also prices per users vary.

— Reviewed by Electronic Resources Committee in some cases.

— It might, if we had to be concerned about various choices of user interface or compatibility issues.

— Yes. More background research and consultation prior to ordering to determine technical requirements, and license restrictions (if any).

— Yes, would want trial period before making purchasing decision.

— The only difference would be the necessity of consulting with the head of our computer department to be sure that we could use the program.

— Technology coordinator for district would be involved if the material was networked.

— Online ref. databases are selected jointly with library directors at other CMC library sites.

— Normally and currently, the Director decides on on-line databases with state-wide consortium. Also software & CD products, sometimes with staff advice.

— No—all P.O.s have to be signed at a higher level.

— Yes—need library committee approval.

— We go through a checking process to determine hardware availability, software and other compatibility and housing decisions.

— Yes, not different for monographs (e.g., CDs). Continuing subscriptions (e.g., journals, indexes) have entirely separate process.

— Not sure

— All affected areas must be aware of the purchase: collection development, reference, serials, and systems.

— Yes. Requires Committee review. Requires input by systems staff and review of legal requirements.

— Licensing agreements require more consultation during the acquisition process.

— Sometimes decisions concerning large purchases are made by a committee.

— It would not differ.

— We purchase these through out state consortium with a committee making recommendations—i.e., we're moving IAC to EBSCO 1-1-99 because the committee recommendation was adopted.

— Selected by committee.

— Other departments within the library are involved. The public service agencies and automated services departments work with collection management to select electronic products.

— Library Director's approval is required.

— If purchased at a consortia level.

— Yes, the license agreement needs to be studied first, and then, the system needs to indicate whether or not the product can be easily used.

— Instead of individual order from branch, use central committee recommendation for online resources.

— On occasion, acquisitions may be arranged by the Head of Collection Development, but all contracts, licenses, etc. are copied and retained in Acquisition.

Open Ended Responses to Questionnaire
Please feel free to comment further on any questions or problems that were dealt with in this questionnaire.

— We are limited in methods of purchasing and ordering by the school systems policies on orders, previews, etc.

— Telemarketing is a nuisance during busy days. Sales reps. who make appointments prior to visits are more welcome.

— All orders in our facility must go through administrations (2 levels) & then through the business office to cut a purchase order after both levels of admin. have approved requisition. At this point in time, this makes electronic ordering all but impossible.

— Our library HATES, DETESTS, and absolutely DESPISES telemarketing calls. Vendors (and publishers) who make these belong in the lowest level of Hell. And the same goes for advertising e-mail.

— Questionnaire was too time-consuming!

— Our library was rebuilt, so we are "new" but "old." We are strictly limited as to when we may spend the budget money, even down to what month. The library handles book and magazines, etc. Non-Print, such as videos, are ordered through each discipline's dept. chair, then sent to the library for processing and storage.

— Way too much detail and very time consuming. Why not send one type of survey to large libraries and one to medium and small?

— Interesting questions. Some questions made me think about how I was doing things at the library.

— Our library has been searching for a director for 18 months. During this time, the Public Services Librarian has done collection development and for the past 4 months the head cataloger has. For this reason we could not answer many of your questions. Those which were answered are from the Acquisition Librarian and the Head Cataloger.

— Our college is part of a 10 college district. All purchasing is done through our district officer. The college selects the materials to be ordered, inputs the orders on our automated acquisition component of our computerized library system. The district office then places the orders with the publishers & vendors. This includes serials and online products as well. (We really only do the selection at our site. This is the reason I could not respond to a number of the questions). Also, I personally find telemarketing to be a great time-waster. I don't order over the phone & request that the telemarketers send print info through the mail about their products!

— Not sure of the use of some terms such as print monographs & multimedia. We do not have any treatises in our collection & I assumed that was your meaning of print monographs.

— This survey is about 12 pages too long.

— Policy does not allow this library to purchase from telemarketing. College B.O. (business office?) requires all purchase requests go to his office prior to being mailed (surface or electronic).

— I'm a beginning librarian. I'm just learning the ropes. I'm not sure how well my answers reflect reality.

— Right now we are required to pay w/credit cards (procurement cards) whenever possible; therefore, this is very important to me. I ask this question before placing any orders. If the publisher/vendor will not bill with the shipment, and then let me call and pay for the invoice with a credit card—normally I will NOT use that publisher/vendor.

— Vendors rarely visit. When they do, I do not know in advance and therefore, I usually do not purchase from them because I don't know what I need or if my monies are spent.

— I resent publishers' sale persons refusing me access to Web sites unless I take time to talk to them first. I also encourage sales persons to mail me info instead of telling me. Often they are not interested.

— This form is too long.

— None of this applies to us.

— We are a small library—population: 1,800. Many questions do not apply to our small library that has no automated system.

— Questionnaire too long—it was difficult to find the time to fit this in.

— Do it (survey) electronically on web.

— Questionnaire much too long & many questions required guesses— no way to know the real answer.

— I believe that many (most) school districts do not allow direct ordering, as P. O. must be completed & approved before orders are sent. This slows down the process considerably. Without a district librarian, we have no way of pooling orders for better savings.

— I work in a High School District of 14 schools and most of the Librarians, including myself, have abandoned CD–ROM online services for Internet Access Services.

— I feel that I'm doing two jobs for the pay of one position. I'm the media specialist in 2 different buildings, K–6 and 7–12. Each day, I teach consumer Economics, reading classes, and computer classes. This leaves me little time to learn new ideas that are available to media specialists.

— This (survey) was way too long and boring.

— Too long of a survey.

— Almost total dependence on jobber & professional reviews. Extremely small library.

— Your issues dealt mainly with issues from the seller's point of view, ignoring other issues from the buyer's point of view, i.e., cash flow, invoicing, payment methods. Such would probably give insight to the sellers.

— We are a small rural school—what works best for us may not always be standard library protocol.

— Because this is a very small library, many questions did not apply to us. Unavoidable.

— I think the questions needed some explanation or context. What is it that you are trying to find out? Your questions mix several situations together. My answers for electronic vendors & publications might differ from those for print & video.

— Our relations with both vendors & publishers are satisfactory. We are happy (generally) with their services as long as they don't call us on the telephone about new products & services.

— I hate telemarketers who try to talk when I've told them to mail their offers. I don't have the time for them!!

— The survey was too long. I hope it is useful. Question 53: I do not know what these [ordering formats] are. Explain. I order from Baker & Taylor as needed.

— Surveys requiring this amount of time MUST be of some practical value to libraries!!!

— I'm under a tight time frame. I'm sorry I couldn't give more thought in answering your questionnaire. I hope it is SOME help.

— We hate salesmen calling us, but we must admit that we do buy some things from them. I like to see the books, but it would be better to have:
  A. ONE big catalog from each company,
  B. ANNOTATED (including reviews from school tools—Booklist, etc.) entries,
  C. Pictures when possible,
  D. Return policy that allows previews,
  E. LOWEST POSSIBLE PRICES.

— DON'T SEND MULTIPLE COPIES OF SAME CATALOG. (PLEASE TELL THE BOOK COMPANIES WHAT WE LIKE AND DON'T LIKE. IT WILL HAVE BEEN WORTH FILLING OUT THIS FORM).

— I wish vendors and publishers would not visit or call me. I don't have time during the school day to see or talk to them. They need to send me their catalogs and flyers. I will look at them when I have the time.

— I have had to stop receiving calls from telemarketers because I could spend my whole day doing nothing but talking to telemarketers! Pre-processing of library materials is in little use by our library, but is an area we hope to pursue more in the future.

— We are a very small, very specialized library. We hope to grow in the next 5 years and then, perhaps this vendor info. will be used.

— When I get calls from publishers it can be very disruptive to my classes. If they do call I appreciate the ones who say "I have some brochures I will send you on this or that" instead of explaining each one on the phone. Then I am more likely to look for the brochure.

— This questionnaire was too long & many questions were poorly worded. The option of Not Applicable was necessary, but ignored. Publishers & their reps. are a necessary evil, many times.

— I concur with my colleague's remarks. If I had had any idea how long this would take, I wouldn't have started it.

— Many of these questions do not apply to smaller libraries. Our budget is under $30,000 to buy books & other materials and to maintain our building. The library board handles all financial items for this. My book budget for all purchases (audios, videos & magazines is only $6,500. Some years, I purchase more of 1 of these [audios, videos, magazines]. It is a good little library that serves over 12,000 town & rural patrons.

— [Survey] too long.

— This [survey] is unreasonably long!

— Publishers and vendors must realize that when they advertise their books in a catalog, they need to include the following for each book: colorful book cover, paging, copyright date, annotations, and a list of awards. The above criteria helps librarians with the collection process and saves them a lot of time.

— Very lengthy questionnaire.

— Baker & Taylor fill rate is poor. We used a local book vendor but they have gone out of business. We are trying Amazon, but seems expensive . . . next will try Barnes & Noble.

— The survey was much too long!

— I must have misplaced the form — Please send me a free copy.

— Very long and took efforts of 4 department heads. Need longer time line given this was received 11/23/98.

— Survey is too long & time consuming!

— The library budget for this year includes $57,000, which are funds recently approved and allocated by the state. This money has not yet been spent and will be a variable amount each year.

—I found this questionnaire exhaustive and feel that the responses of a library, managed by one certified librarian, will provide little significant data. Also, the thoroughness of this survey prevented my finishing it very promptly.

— Sorry for the delay in returning. Different people filled out different parts.

— This was a very confusing questionnaire.

Bibliography

"The Library Market: A Special PW Survey." *Publishers Weekly* 207, no. 24 (June 16, 1975): 41–68 (eight contributions by various authors on the 1975 survey).

Dessauer, John P. "Library Periodical Acquisitions: A Correction." *Publishers Weekly* 208, no. 19 (November 10, 1975): 26.

———. *Library Acquisitions: A Look into the Future.* New York: Book Industry Group, 1976. (Research Report: Book Industry Study Group, No. 3)

———. "Library Acquisitions by Two Year Colleges: A Look into the Future." *Publishers Weekly* 209, no. 7 (February 16, 1976): 55–58.

———. *A Report on Book Industry Information Needs: Based on a Survey: Conducted for the Book Industry Study Group, Inc.* (Darien, Conn.: s.n., 1976).

Edelman, Hendrik, and Karen Muller. "A New Look at the Library Market." *Publishers Weekly* 231, no. 21 (May 29, 1987): 30–35 (report of the 1986 AAP/ALA survey, a repeat of the 1975 survey—the actual data were not published).

Dessauer, John P., and Thomas Leven. *Library Acquisition Survey: 1988.* New York: Center for Book Research, 1988 (a repeat of the 1975 survey).

Index

Abel, Richard. *See* Richard Abel Company
Academic Book Center, 40
academic libraries, 6, 8–10, 14, 20, 22–27, 38–40, 45, 59–61, 70
acquisitions and mergers. *See* mergers and acquisitions
acquisitions budget. *See* library materials budget
ACQNET, 28
AcqWeb, 28, 47, 48
Advance, 62
Alabaster, Carol, 44
Amazon.com, 16–17, 28, 31, 40, 52–57, 61, 63, 67, 75
Ambassador Book Service, vi
American Library Association (ALA), Annual Conference, vi, 19, 38, 66, 79, 81
approval plans, 11, 14, 16, 38–39, 41–42, 59–60, 63, 68
Association for Collection and Library Technical Services (ACLTS), v, vi, 3, 5, 7, 27
Association of American Publishers (AAP), v, vi, 3, 5, 7, 81
author visits, 44, 50
automation, library. *See* library automation

Bach, Johann Sebastian, 56
back list, 9, 16, 25, 36–37, 42, 48, 50–51, 67
Baker & Taylor, vi, 18, 29, 62
Baltimore County Library, 30
Barnes & Noble, 44, 60
BarnesandNoble.com, 47, 63, 67
Belanger, Janet, 44
Berkeley Publishing Company, 50
Bezos, Jeff, 52
Blackwell's Book Services, vi, 40, 42
blanket orders, 11, 39
Book Expo America (BEA), 22, 30, 66, 69, 79, 81
Book Industry Study Group (BISG), 9, 48
Booking Ahead, 62
Booklife, 47
Booklist, 37, 67
Books in Print, 36, 67, 69
Borders, 60
Bowker. *See* R. R. Bowker
Brandon Hill List, 60
Brill's Content, 31
Brodart Company, vi

Cataloging in Publication (CIP), 4, 13

catalogs, publisher, 11–12, 15, 20, 24, 39, 48–49, 66, 68
Charleston Conference, 38
Charleston Group, vi
children's books, 10, 29
Choice, vi, 28, 37, 67
Christensen, Clint, vi
collection development, 10–11, 20–25, 28, 42, 59–65, 68–69
consortia, 4–5, 10, 14, 16–17, 24, 34, 39, 59–61
Cook, Eleanor, 32, 41
copyright, 23, 25–26, 29, 32
Corrsin, Steve, vi
Crow, Sheryl, 57

Davis, Stanley M., 77
Dewey Decimal System, 34
digital books. *See* electronic books
direct mail, 11
discounts, 13, 24–26, 39, 40–41, 64, 67
discussion lists, 24, 32, 47
Disraeli, Benjamin, 75
Domkoski, David, 44
Drucker, Peter, 76
Dylan, Bob, 56

Edelman, Hendrik, vi, 6, 19, 27
Edupage, 47
electronic books, 17, 20, 22–23, 25, 31, 42, 45, 52, 77
electronic journals, 6, 23, 28, 48
electronic publishers, 8
Entertainment Weekly, 57
exhibits, 11, 12, 19, 29, 30, 36, 38, 66, 76

Ferguson, Anthony, 27, 28, 31–32, 41, 77
Fialkoff, Francine, 76
FirstSearch, 25
Ford, Richard, 30
Friends of Libraries, USA (FOLUSA), vi

Gale Group, vi,
Greenspan, Allen, 53
Grove's Dictionaries, vi

HarperCollins, 69
Henry Holt & Co., vi

IFLA Journal, 4
Ingram Library Services, vi, 18–20, 42, 62
International Coalition of Library Consortia, 24
international rights, 18
International Standard Book Number (ISBN), 4, 13, 51
International Standard Serials Number (ISSN), 4, 13
Internet, 15 17, 20–21, 27, 29, 31–32, 36–37, 40–41, 43, 45, 47–48, 50–52, 55, 58, 62

James, Rebecca, 71
John Wiley & Sons, vii

Karon, Jan, 50
Keeley, Martin, 28, 30

Leiserson, Anna Belle, 28
library automation, 13, 21–22, 27, 73
Library Journal, vi, 16, 19, 28–29, 37, 45, 62, 67
LJ Alert, 62
library materials budget, 9–10, 15, 20–21, 48, 70
licensing, 23, 25–26, 29
Lightning Print, 42
Lundy, Dan, vii, 6

Mayer, Christopher, 77
McCallion, Peter, 68
McGraw-Hill, vi
market research, 12, 19
Medlive, 47
Meltzer, Brad, 58

mergers and acquisitions, 8, 19, 28, 40, 50
Midwest Library Service, vi
Muller, Karen, vii, 5

Netlibrary.com, 25, 42, 76
New York Public Library, 47
New York Times, 31, 51, 56–57, 67
New York Times Book Review, 67
Nuis, Aad, 4

OCLC, 3
OhioLINK, 60
order placement, 12–13, 16–17, 21–22, 27–28, 35, 37–39, 48, 59–65, 68
Oryx Press, 41
out-of-print books, 16–17, 25, 42
outsourcing, 14, 19–20, 36, 64
Ovid, 25
Oxford University Press, vi, 17

paperbacks, 4, 10, 22, 32
Pasteur, Louis, 58
Penguin Putnam, vi, 6, 49–50, 63, 77
Penguinclassics.com, 50–51
Phoenix Public Library, 44
Picasso, Pablo, 54
pricing. *See* discounts
public libraries, 8–10, 14, 20, 23, 27, 29, 35–37, 40, 44, 61–65, 68
publishers catalogs. *See* catalogs, publisher
Publishers Weekly, vi, 28–30, 37, 67
Publive, 47
Purcell, Marci, 69
Pushkin, Alexander, 51
PW Daily, 47, 63

Queens Borough Public Library, 61–62

Random House, vi, 17, 69
Rawlinson, Nora, 79

returns, 13
reviews, 4, 11, 16, 22, 24, 27, 30, 36, 43–45, 48, 57–58, 65–68
Richard Abel Company, 2
Rocket E-book, 31, 52
Rodriguez, Michael, vi
Rooney, Robert, 45
R. R. Bowker, vi, 69

sales calls, 11, 26, 38–39, 41–42, 63–64, 66, 68, 71–73
Saporan, Fred, 29
School Library Journal, vi
school media center libraries, 8–10, 14, 23, 27, 69
Seattle Public Library, 68
Seger, Rebecca, vii
Silver Platter, 25
SKP Associates, vii
SoftBook, 52
special libraries, 8–9
Sprout, 42
Stanley, Virginia, 69
Steckler, Phyllis, 41
STM, 8, 25

Tacoma Public Library, 44
Tae Bo, 55
telemarketing, 4–5, 11, 12, 37–38, 66, 71
Ten Speed Press, 3
Thieme Verlag, 25
Time Magazine, 30
Tolstoy, Leo, 51
trade shows. *See* American Library Association (ALA), Annual Conference; Book Expo America (BEA); exhibits
Trow, George W. S., 53

Ulsamer, James, 18, 27
University of Delaware, 27
Utah Academic Library Consortium, 59–61

vendor visits. *See* sales calls
Viking Press, 50
Vonnegut, Kurt, 32

Ward, Artemus, 75
Washington Post, 53
Web. *See* Internet
Whittaker, Martha, 77

Wiley. *See* John Wiley & Sons
Winfrey, Oprah, 32, 48

Yankee Book Peddler, vii
Young, Neil, 55
Young, Phyllis, 30, 41

Zeidner, Lisa, 63

About the Contributors

Rick Ayre is currently a consultant. At the time of the conference, he was vice president and executive editor at Amazon.com. He remains an avid reader.

Janet Belanger is head of the Acquisitions Department at Northeastern University Libraries. She previously worked in the Collection Development and Evaluation Section (CODES) of the Boston Public Library. She was chair of the Policy and Planning Committee in the acquisitions section of ALCTS and served on the Union List of Serials Committee, Serials Sections, Association for Library Collections and Technical Services (ALCTS).

Eleanor Cook is the coordinator of serials and the interim coordinator of acquisitions for Belk Library, Appalachian State University, Boone, N.C. She is the current editor of ACQNET-L, an electronic list devoted to discussion of issues in library acquisitions. She is active in the ALCTS and the North American Serials Group.

Kathleen Cotter is the coordinator of collection development at Queens Borough Public Library. She was the assistant coordinator in the Office of Materials Selection at Brooklyn Public Library and a collection development specialist at Baker and Taylor. She has been active in the CODES Section of the Reference and User Services Association (RUSA).

Yvette Berthel Diven is the director of online and site license services at R. R. Bowker, where she is principally responsible for establishing and maintaining Bowker's vendor partner relationships. Over the past seven years, she has built relationships with a wide spectrum of library automation vendors and database access providers who make Bowker databases available through their systems to individual libraries, library networks, statewide consortia, and international sites.

Hendrik Edelman recently retired from the faculty of the Department of Library and Information Science at Rutgers University after forty years in the international book trade, academic librarianship, and library education. He is continuing his many consulting, research, and teaching activities.

Anthony W. Ferguson was the associate university librarian, Columbia University, at the time of the conference. He recently accepted the position of librarian at the University of Hong Kong.

Francine Fialkoff is editor of the *Library Journal* (*LJ*) and writes "Inside Track," a column on issues in reviewing and the library/publisher connection. Before becoming editor of *LJ*, she was that magazine's book review editor. She is a member of the executive board of Friends of Libraries USA (FOLUSA) and of Libraries for the Future and is one of the judges for the newly created *New York Times* library awards.

Robert P. Holley is a professor of library and information science, Wayne State University, where he also served as interim dean and associate dean during this period. He is the ALCTS cochair of the Association of American Publishers (AAP) and ALCTS Joint Committee. Before coming to Wayne State University, he held positions at the University of Utah and Yale University.

Rebecca James joined the Ingram Library Services staff in December 1995 as the director of sales. She was named vice president of sales and marketing in 1996 and previously served in various positions at Baker and Taylor. She gained frontline library experience at the Franklin public schools, South Milwaukee Public Library, and Racine Unified Schools, all in Wisconsin.

Marty Keely is the president and chief executive officer of Ingram Library Services and Ingram International and is very active in professional library activities. He currently serves as the vice president of the FOLUSA and is a strong advocate for the Fund for Libraries.

Dan Lundy is the vice president of academic sales at Penguin Putnam Inc. He has been responsible for marketing all the company's adult titles to library, academic, and educational audiences. He is a member of the AAP Trade Libraries Committee and the AAP cochair of the AAP/ALCTS Joint Committee.

Peter McCallion retired from the New York Public Library where he was the head of acquisitions for the Branch Libraries and was responsible for purchasing more than one million items each year. He has served on library marketing advisory boards for many publishers and various committees, including chairing the AAP/ALCTS Joint Committee.

Peter McCarthy is the director of Penguin Putnam Online, the Web-marketing and new media publishing department of the U.S.–operating company of the Penguin Group. Prior to joining Penguin Putnam, he was the associate director of electronic publishing for the *New York Review of Books* and *Granta*. He also served as the senior editor for the second edition of the *Readers Catalog*.

Sarah Michalak is the director of the J. Willard Marriott Library at the University of Utah. Prior to her appointment as director in 1995, she held positions at the University of Washington Libraries and the University of California, Riverside. She chairs the Utah Academic Library Consortium Directors Council, as well as the Building and Equipment Section of ALA's Library Administration and Management Association, and is a founding member of the Association of Research Libraries' Scholarly Publishing and Academic Resources Coalition (SPARC) Working Group.

Karen Muller was the executive director of ALCTS/LAMA, two divisions of the American Library Association (ALA), at the time of the conference. She recently accepted the position of librarian and knowledge manager within the ALA.

Nancy Pearl is the director of the Washington Center for the Book at the Seattle Public Library. She is the author of *Now Read This: A Guide to Mainstream Fiction, 1978–1998*. She was the chair of the ALA Notable Books Council, the Readers' Advisory Committee, and the Collection Development Discussion Group. In 1998, she was *Library Journal*'s Fiction Reviewer of the Year.

Alice Peery was most recently the collection management director of the Public Library of Charlotte and Mecklenburg County, N.C. She was responsible for the system-wide collection management of a public library system with a central library, five regional libraries, and fifteen branch libraries that circulated over six million items per year with a materials budget of over $3 million.

Eugenie Prime is the manager of Corporate Libraries at Hewlett Packard Company. Before joining Hewlett-Packard, she was the president of CINAHL Corporation, a publisher and database producer of the *Index to Nursing* and *Allied Health Literature*. She speaks extensively in the areas of information management, digital libraries, strategic planning, and knowledge management.

Nora Rawlinson is the editor in chief of *Publishers Weekly*, a position she has held since 1992. She had previously served as editor of *Library Journal* and as the head of materials selection of the Baltimore County Public Library. She remains active in the ALA and has served on the RUSA/CODE Book Review Committee.

Robert Rooney began his career over twenty years ago as a bookseller. Since then he has been a publishers sales representative with W. H. Smith and the director of sales with Chelsea House. He joined Taylor and Francis thirteen years ago, and for the last ten years he has been the vice president of sales and marketing.

Patricia Schroeder is the president and chief executive officer of the AAP. She served in Congress for twelve terms and left the House of Representatives undefeated in 1996. She held the rank of professor at the Woodrow Wilson School of Public and International Affairs at Princeton University before assuming her post at the AAP in 1997.

Rebecca Seger is the director of library and academic sales and marketing for the McGraw-Hill Professional Book Group. Previously, she has worked in various positions at HarperCollins, Penguin, and Elsevier Science. She is currently chair of the AAP Libraries Committee, cochair of the AAP/ALCTS Joint Committee, and serves on the Publishers Committee of the FOLUSA.

James S. Ulsamer is the executive vice president of Baker and Taylor, Inc., and the president of Baker and Taylor Books. He serves on the board of various organizations including the Book Industry Study Group and Varsitybooks.com. He is also a member of the Board of Visitors of the School of Information and Library Science, University of North Carolina at Chapel Hill.

Martha Whittaker became the vice president of marketing for Blackwell's Book Services in 1999 when Blackwell purchased Academic Book Center, where she held a similar position. Previously, she was a vice president of the CARL Corporation and general manager of CARL's subsidiary, the UnCover Company.

Phyllis Young is the collection development coordinator for the County of Los Angeles Public Library, one of the largest urban libraries in the United States. She works with a team of regional collection coordinators/subject specialists and material evaluators to select materials in all formats to be added to the library's collections. She is active in both RUSA and ALCTS.